Contents

MARKETING FURTHER AND HIGHER EDUCATION — A Handbook

Peter Davies
Further Education Unit

Keith Scribbins
Further Education Staff College

with drawings by

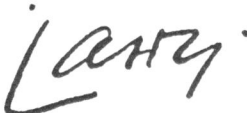

Longman for

The Authors

Peter Davies is a Development Officer of the Further Education Unit. He is a graduate of St. John's College, Cambridge, where he read Economics and History. From 1969-77 he worked for British Rail, for most of this period as a marketing assistant to one of BR's inter-city service group managers. In 1976 he obtained an M.Sc. (Administrative Sciences) at City University, majoring in Marketing. From 1977 to 1984 he was an officer firstly of the Business Education Council (BEC) and then the Business and Technician Education Council (BTEC).

Keith Scribbins is a Staff Tutor at the Further Education Staff College. Educated at the University of London and Sussex University he taught in further education colleges in London and Worcester prior to working, from 1973 to 1983, for the National Association of Teachers in Further and Higher Education where he specialised in salary negotiations and employment law. He has acted as a consultant to a number of LEAs, colleges and other organisations, both in this country and abroad, on areas including industrial relations, public relations and marketing.

© Further Education Unit (FEU) and Further Education Staff College (FESC) 1985.
Published on behalf of the Further Education Unit and Further Education Staff College by Longman Group Ltd.

First published 1985.

Printed in Great Britain by Longman Group Resources Unit,
62 Hallfield Road, York YO3 7XQ.

Acknowledgements

Without the work of some colleagues this publication would not have been possible. In particular, Section I owes a great deal to David Ford, Senior Lecturer in Marketing at Bath University; comments on overseas markets, which appear in Sections 2, 3, and 4 are based on information supplied by Lynton Gray, Senior Lecturer at North East London Polytechnic; the paragraphs on pricing in Section 3 draw on material produced by Graham Robinson (Director of Wigan College Management Centre) in conjunction with PICKUP Conferences; the paragraphs on using the media in Section 4 are based on a talk given by Paula Lanning, NATFHE's Information Officer, to a conference held at the Further Education Staff College in July 1984; others parts of Section 4 owe much to the work of Martyn Davis, Head of Marketing Services at The College for the Distributive Trades. Without the help of Bill Easton, Principal of Southgate Technical College, David Moore, Principal, Nelson and Colne College, Mike Pascoe, Publicity Officer, Bristol Polytechnic and Brenda Remington, Principal, Haringey College, some of the examples cited in the text would not have been available to us. Russ Curtis, Lecturer at The British Columbia Institute of Technology, also gave us valuable material on marketing in general and the promotion of his institution in particular.

Special thanks must go to Rob Cuthbert, Staff Tutor, The Further Education Staff College, whose work in developing marketing courses and associated learning material at the Staff College since 1979 considerably informed our text.

We would also like to acknowledge the support of John Cassels, Director General of the National Economic Development Council, and Sandra Newton, formerly of the Manpower Services Commission, who encouraged us in the production of this handbook.

Jack Mansell, the Chief Officer of the Further Education Unit, and Gordon Wheeler, the former Director of the Further Education Staff College, together agreed on the original idea for the production of this handbook. They also gave us considerable support in its preparation, as did Geoffrey Melling, the present Director of FESC. We also acknowledge the assistance of FEU's Education Management Advisory Committee.

The following provided us with some very helpful criticisms of earlier drafts of the handbook.

A. Albrecht, Principal, Basford Hall College; D. Birch, Deputy

Director, Further Education Staff College; M. Bone, Head of Department, South Bristol Technical College; D. Brooks, Vice-Principal, Ystrad Mynach College of Further Education; H. Buls, Assistant Principal, Tameside College of Technology; A. Cass, Principal, Wearside College of Further Education; R. Challis, Staff Tutor, Further Education Staff College; D. Chowdhury, Associate Tutor, Further Education Staff College; D. Drysdale, Deputy Chief Officer, Further Education Unit; N. Ellidge, Regional Development Agent, PICKUP; R. Finn, Head of Short Course Unit, Mid-Kent College; M. French, Manpower Services Commission; R. Flude, Head of Department, Melton Mowbray College of Further Education; J. Geale, Regional Development Agent, PICKUP; R. Griffin, Principal, Lancaster and Morecambe College of Further Education; Sir Roy Harding, formerly Chief Education Officer, Buckinghamshire County Council; L. Hough, Principal, Halton College of Further Education; M. Hughes, Vice-Principal, Nelson and Colne College; R. Kedney, Senior Assistant Director of Further Education, City of Liverpool; J. Latcham, Associate Tutor, Further Education Staff College; M. Leech, Principal, Harrow College of Further Education; M. McAllister, Principal, Blackpool and Fylde College of Further and Higher Education; I. McNay, the Open University; A. Parker, Vice-Principal, Lancaster and Morecambe College of Further Education; D. Parkes, Staff Tutor, Further Education Staff College; Sir Alan Richmond, Associate Tutor, Further Education Staff College; A. Shaw, Principal, Longlands College of Further Education; J. Sprigg, the Audit Commission; I. Waitt, Senior Lecturer, North East London Polytechnic; P. Webb, Her Majesty's Inspectorate.

We are grateful to South West Regional Management Centre for permission to quote from and adapt some of the material from B. Cawthray's helpful manual 'Putting it Together: Marketing and Advertising', published by the Centre in 1982, and to Prentice/Hall International Inc. for allowing us to use the quotations from P. Kotler's 'Marketing Management — Analysis, Planning and Control'.

Our thanks also go to 'Larry' for his splendid cartoons.

Finally, we are grateful to all the typists who struggled through the redrafts of our text. Any failings do, of course, remain our own.

Peter Davies
Further Education Unit

Keith Scribbins
Further Education Staff College

Foreword

The need for an improvement in the marketing capabilities of the further education service has rapidly become part of the conventional wisdom. The adverse and simplistic criticisms of education's lack of responsiveness to the needs of 'U.K. Ltd.' are, like most generalisations, often unfair. It is obvious that some parts of the FE system have an established reputation for responsiveness. However, some of the criticisms cannot be ignored and today FE is being held more and more accountable for its ability to meet market needs.

This handbook provides some basic guidance on the possible responses to this challenge. Its authors argue against the notion that marketing is not a respectable activity for educationalists. They also demonstrate that marketing involves much more than merely selling an existing range of services. Both FEU and FESC endorse these opinions.

The handbook argues that a marketing perspective offers a coherent framework which can relate to many features of the current FE scene. Few readers will be totally unfamiliar with the strategies described in the following pages, and the basic concepts of marketing are not in themselves complicated. The primary importance which marketing gives to the customer's viewpoint does, however, present a timely challenge to the view that 'teacher knows best'. There is a great deal here for college and LEA staff to learn.

Whilst not many people within the system have talked hitherto of marketing, increasing numbers are recognising the validity of 'the responsive college', 'student-centred curricula' and 'flexible delivery systems'. Marketing *is* taking place, but more often than not unconsciously: this is reflected in the lack of clearly identified corporate marketing objectives for colleges, co-ordinated systems and procedures, and adequate resourcing specifically allocated to this function.

The demands for greater accountability and responsiveness in education, coupled with the absence of a statutory base for the FE sector, whilst perhaps threatening, have nevertheless created an awareness of the need for a more coherent and committed approach to marketing. This handbook demonstrates that marketing concepts and techniques present FE with significant opportunities. An accent on the positive benefits of marketing, rather than the dangers of standing aloof from it, is likely to gain more long-term commitment from staff to the changes in systems and procedures which may be required as a consequence.

It is a thesis of the handbook that the marketing perspective is an agent for change: change which will affect LEAs as well as colleges and may call for considerable reforms in the funding of provision in further and higher education, the methods of curriculum delivery, the duties required of staff and, hence, the present system for regulating the working arrangements for staff and the grading of their posts. The handbook therefore contains clear messages for LEAs, as well as for colleges.

The Further Education Staff College and the Further Education Unit have both recognised the need to provide support to FE staff who wish to develop their marketing capabilities. FESC has been offering successfully, for some years, a 'Marketing Courses' module within its 'Management in Colleges' conference series, and has also produced a number of papers on the subject. The FEU, in the belief that curriculum change and education management are inextricably linked, is currently funding a number of projects in order to promote and evaluate the effects of more thoroughgoing marketing approaches in colleges. The complementary nature of this work provides one reason for FESC and FEU jointly publishing this handbook. Another is our joint concern to demonstrate that solutions to the problems of relating further and higher education to changes in market needs can be generated from within the FE service. Finally, both FESC and FEU aim to introduce the concepts and techniques of marketing to as wide an audience as possible and to establish marketing as part of staff development in further and higher education.

We are sure the handbook will provide a useful introduction to marketing in further and higher education and we will be pleased to receive suggestions for ways in which our organisations can assist further in the dissemination of the advice contained within it.

Jack Mansell
Chief Officer
Further Education Unit

Geoffrey Melling
Director
Further Education Staff College

Introduction

This handbook is intended as a source of guidance on marketing concepts and techniques and their application in further and higher education. It is designed not only for college managers, but for all staff in the FHE system, including course tutors, support staff and LEA officers, who are involved in marketing the products of FHE. It is the outcome of collaboration between the Further Education Staff College and the Further Education Unit (a full acknowledgement of the sources which have been drawn upon is given on p. vi).

The handbook is intended to provide a source of reference to be consulted by staff at all levels as and when the need arises for advice on specific aspects of marketing. A synopsis of what follows is provided at the beginning of each of the Sections 1-4 as an aid to the easy identification of the relevant details. It is not envisaged that the handbook will be read from cover to cover, although its authors believe that the text follows a logical order and can be read sequentially. The wallet back cover is intended to allow for the insertion of supplementary information concerning college procedures, local market intelligence and so on. It is hoped that the handbook will provide a source of support material for staff development workshops and conferences concerning the marketing of the FHE service.

Section 1 is concerned with setting the scene: it outlines the basics of marketing theory and the nature of the FHE market. As such it is mainly concerned with underlying concepts and principles rather than practical techniques. Those staff familiar with marketing concepts and with the current FHE system may well find it more useful to go straight to the areas which interest them in the other sections. Other staff are recommended to take the trouble to read Section 1 first, as the detailed applications of marketing techniques are likely to prove more effective if they are based on an understanding and acceptance of the underlying concepts. Section 2 deals with marketing research and Sections 3 and 4 with the four p's of marketing, product, place (i.e. delivery), price and promotion. Section 3 also examines the implications of marketing for college organisational structures. Section 4 is given over entirely to promotion, since this is an area of marketing where a large number of practical techniques can be applied effectively at college level by a wide range of staff. Guidance on further sources of relevant information is given in Section 5.

Marketing is far easier to write about than to put into practice: the handbook does not pretend to contain all the answers, and should be seen as containing starting points rather than a set of procedures to be rigidly followed. There is evidence that many colleges and LEAs are already becoming alive to the relevance of marketing concepts and techniques. Marketing is being seen to have an important contribution to make to the corporate strategy of LEAs and colleges, and as having important implications for the relationships between LEAs and colleges in terms of the framework in which the latter operate. It is hoped that the handbook will provide additional support for the marketing of the FHE system, and a stimulus for continued staff development in this area.

1. Marketing and Further Education

Synopsis

This introductory section considers the debates about the **relevance** of marketing to further and higher education and about the **quality** of the sector's marketing approaches.

The recent criticisms of FHE's marketing, from the Government and the Audit Commission amongst others, are outlined, as are the many longer standing criticisms of the narrow appeal of FHE, which can also be seen as criticisms of its marketing. The justification for these claims is examined, as is the counter-argument that marketing is not a 'respectable' pursuit for educationalists. This view is dismissed in favour of the idea that if properly understood, organised and reviewed, the marketing perspective can have a radical effect on the work of colleges and LEAs.

Some key **concepts** from marketing theory are outlined briefly. These include the idea that for any product or service a **marketing mix** can be developed on the basis of the product itself, its price, its place of delivery and its promotion. For any product or service it will be necessary to define a **target market** which can be classified by such criteria as the objects the market wishes to buy, the occasions when it wishes to do so, and the personnel or groups who are involved in the purchase. The idea that all products or services undergo a **life cycle** is introduced and the fact that any market consists of a number of **market segments** is explained. The importance which an organisation assigns to marketing is reflected in the resources allocated to it and the **staffing** arrangements made for it. In recent years **social marketing** has been studied specifically. This is seen to have implications for the way in which public awareness about FHE may be raised, and its image improved.

Some of the difficulties in and opportunities for **applying these concepts** to FHE, and a marketing perspective based on them, are then examined. The multiplicity of a college's publics, the diversification of control within the system, the variety of objectives which the LEA and colleges may have, the nature of the growing competition and the external constraints operating on colleges and LEAs are identified as the characteristic features of FHE of which any marketing perspective must take account.

A marketing perspective is then examined as a stimulus for a range of changes in the organisation and delivery of FHE.

The section ends with a suggested framework for a **marketing audit** which is seen as a necessary preliminary to drawing up a marketing plan. The **'portfolio', or 'Boston', matrix** is suggested as a useful analytical concept for establishing the relative position of courses within their overall market.

Is marketing relevant to FE?

Pressures exist both inside and outside further education for it to take marketing more seriously. Some of these pressures are new.

- The Audit Commission has drawn attention to the inefficient marketing approaches of FE.
- The Government's White Paper *Training for Jobs* criticises FE's failure to market itself effectively.
- HMIs have pointed to unimaginative promotion of courses and colleges.

Some of the pressures are not so new:

- For many years commentators have criticised the narrowness of the traditional FE market pointing out that some sectors of our population (e.g. women, ethnic minorities, the unemployed, those over 21) have been neglected by the service.
- Criticisms of the narrow skill orientation or much of the traditional FE curriculum also represent a criticism of FE's failure to know its potential market and that market's changing needs.
- There is evidence to suggest that the general public is far more ignorant of the existence of the FHE system, and of the variety of provision which it makes, than it is about the secondary or university sectors.
- Inevitably, there will be a perennial argument about the 'mission' of further and higher education (FHE) and its institutions, given that this sector of education is not mandatory and is under increasing pressure as far as resources are concerned. Hence, the persistence in FHE of arguments about the appropriateness of aiming at one market segment rather than another.

Whether or not these criticisms are fully or partially justified, they have been made in several instances by those who will shape the future development of further education and training in the UK.

Against them it has to be said that FHE has shown itself to be more adaptable to customer needs than many other parts of the education and training system. It has had a degree of market orientation and in some cases it has established good links with local employers, with community groups, schools and other agencies. Given the budgets allocated to marketing, some colleges have produced exciting literature, novel promotional techniques and successful advertising. It is not the point of this handbook to praise or blame the FHE system in respect of its marketing, but rather to provide some guidance on marketing processes and their relevance to all colleges whether or not they have in the past developed a strategy for marketing their provision.

Marketing is very easy to talk about — its concepts and theories can be easily grasped — but rather difficult to do. If this is true of marketing a commodity, the production of which is motivated by a search for profit and need to sell, it is dramatically true of marketing a social service such as education. Indeed, the very idea that education should be marketed is foreign to many and may be offensive to some within the education profession. There are some deep roots of objection to the notion that education, any more than medicine or law, should be presented to the public via the slick techniques associated with the advertising, packaging and selling of commercial products. Indeed, some philosophies of the purpose and nature of education are distinctly anti-marketing.

'The intellectual has never felt kindly toward the market place: to him it has always been a place of vulgar men and base motives.' Stigler, G. S. *The Intellectual and the Market Place.* Institute of Economic Affairs Occasional Paper, 1963.

In areas in which student recruitment is buoyant and restricted only by the Government's willingness to match resources to need, it is tempting to conclude that the market is artificially supressed. Equally, some will argue that expert and trained professionals know what kind of education to provide for the population: they are there to establish and maintain standards, not to respond to the passing whims of governments, employers or the public. The professionals, this argument runs, know best. Indeed, those who reject the idea that marketing is relevant to education point to the reputation of Britain's education system and its courses as the product of generations of development: a product whose quality speaks for itself.

Ultimately these arguments are irrelevant for no matter how much truth there may be in the camps of those who propose and oppose the notion that marketing perspectives have something to offer further education, the fact is that colleges, polytechnics and universities do market themselves. Their existence entails marketing since they provide a service about which, at the very least, they have to notify the public. Furthermore, it is required by law (Education Act 1980) that schools produce brochures indicating their activities and facilities. There is in FHE no such thing as no marketing: its marketing is either good or bad, successful or unsuccessful. Indeed, as we shall see, the idea that the service exists to cater for some need, or to pursue some goal of academic policy, presupposes certain market decisions. In any event the notion that FHE provides a quality product which does not need marketing fails to recognise that it is the public, or at least sections of it, who makes the judgements which enable the label of quality to be applied. To put it another way, 'quality' is a rather meaningless concept unless it refers to market perceptions.

For all these reasons, and others dealt with in more detail elsewhere in this handbook, the marketing approach is relevant and important to those who manage, administer and teach in the FHE system.

Marketing: Some key concepts

'Colleges facing declining enrolments are now investing heavily in advertising and recruitment activities. But these selling steps turn out to be only stop gap measures. These organisations begin to realise the need to define their target markets more carefully; research their needs, wants and values; modernise their products and programs and communicate more effectively. Such organisations turn from selling to marketing' Kotler, P. *Marketing Management – Analysis, Planning and Control.* Prentice/Hall International Inc, New Jersey, 1980.

Marketing is not just about the tactics of selling. Nor is it just about repackaging old products. Marketing theory starts from the notion of the **marketing mix.** This is simply a convenient way of itemising the general options open to those who provide a service or product.

ILLUSTRATION 1 THE MARKETING MIX: THE FOUR 'Ps'

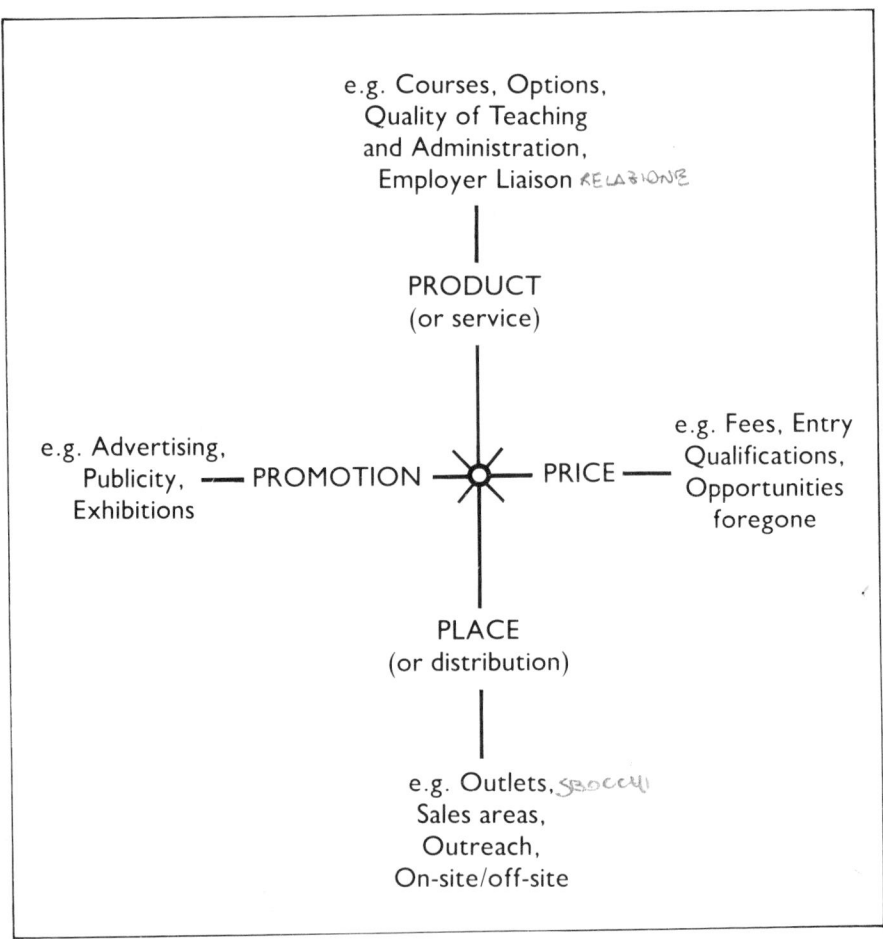

e.g. Courses, Options,
Quality of Teaching
and Administration,
Employer Liaison RELAZIONE

PRODUCT
(or service)

e.g. Advertising, — **PROMOTION** — **PRICE** — e.g. Fees, Entry
Publicity, Qualifications,
Exhibitions Opportunities
foregone

PLACE
(or distribution)

e.g. Outlets, SBOCCHI
Sales areas,
Outreach,
On-site/off-site

Marketing will be most successful when the resources in the mix categories are balanced in the optimum way relevant to that service. For example, in marketing a short course, the entry fee (or price) is likely to be an important ingredient in its success or failure. In the case of a full-time long course, price may be less important than the quality of the course or its promotion and place of operation. In relation to FHE, the place of delivery is becoming more and more significant with recent developments in open learning, off-college schemes and outreach work. The **target market** posits a check-list of questions, the answers to which will assist in the fine tuning of the marketing mix. Most significantly it allows the identification of gaps in the market.

For example, in FHE, individuals, employers, parents and community groups are all involved, separately or together, in the decision to 'purchase' a particular course. The timing of the course may be critical to the target market selected for it. ↳ SCELTA DEL MOMENTO OPPORTUNO

6

ILLUSTRATION 2 THE TARGET MARKET: THE SIX 'Os'

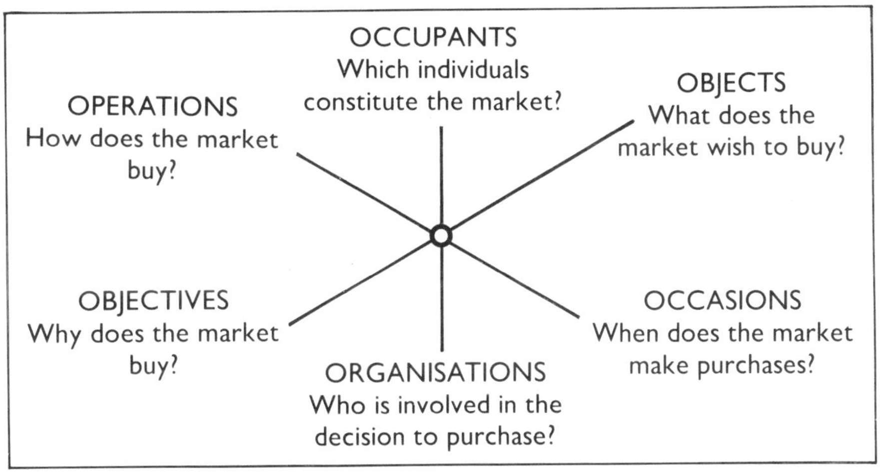

No producers should enter into the market place without **market information.** Marketing research, of which one part is market research, aims to provide, by systematic investigation, knowledge of all factors which impinge on the marketing of goods and services. It embraces market, sales, product, advertising, and motivation research. It can entail expenditure (as with some market research programmes) but can also involve relatively low cost systems of information storage about customer's attitudes to the service offered and their progress within it.

It is a fundamental tenet of marketing that products have a definite **life cycle.** A typical life cycle relates demand to a time continuum dividing the process into stages of introduction, growth, maturity and decline. Some analyses develop the characteristics associated with each stage into complex connections as shown in Illustration 3.

ILLUSTRATION 3 THE PRODUCT LIFE CYCLE

	CHARACTERISTICS			
	INTRO	GROWTH	MATURITY	DECLINE
Sales	Low	Fast growth	Slow growth or stability	Decline
Profits	Negligible	Peak levels	Declining	Low or zero
Cash Flow	Negative	Moderate	High	Low
Customers	Innovative	Mass market	Mass market	Laggards
Competitors	Few	Growing	Many rivals	Declining number
Product differentiation	Considerable (may be unique)	Reducing	Low	Low
Product expenditure	High per unit of sales	High in absolute terms – falling in unit costs	Stable – often modest or even negligible	Defensive and unstable – easily wasted

DEMAND (vertical axis) / TIME (horizontal axis)

Studies of the life cycles of commercial products show that their launch and growth is associated with a relatively gradual rise in demand. Demand is at a peak in their maturity and sharply falls in the decline phase. This process may take place over any period of time from a few weeks to many years, depending on the product. The shape of the sales curve is basically the same, however, and decline is eventually inevitable unless the product is 'relaunched' by changes in at least one of the elements of its marketing mix. The high development costs of the 'introduction' phase are associated with relatively low sales volumes. Any profits are unlikely to arise until the growth stage as promotion and development costs are spread over a large volume of sales. How true this is of products in FHE is difficult to gauge but some research is already underway in this area. The product life cycle concept suggests that there are grave dangers facing any organisation whose product range is weighted towards the 'maturity' and 'decline' stages. Unless action is taken, the future can only bring an overall decline, the newer offerings being insufficient to offset the deterioration.

Market segmentation involves subdividing the market into subsets of customers for whom a distinct marketing mix will be relevant. To be useful the segments should be measurable, accessible and substantial.

ILLUSTRATION 4 DIFFERENT APPROACHES TO MARKET SEGMENTATION

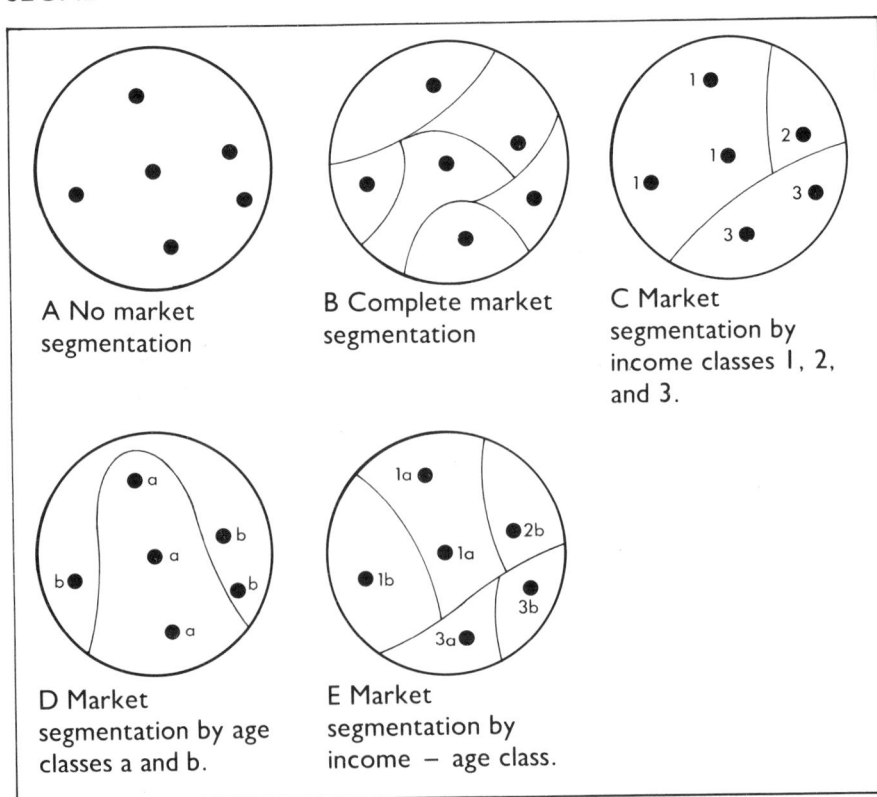

A No market segmentation

B Complete market segmentation

C Market segmentation by income classes 1, 2, and 3.

D Market segmentation by age classes a and b.

E Market segmentation by income – age class.

Source: Kotler, P. Marketing Management – Analysis, Planning and Control. Prentice/Hall International Inc. New Jersey. 1980.

Segmentation is important because it allows needs in the community to be differentiated and catered for. It is unlikely that one product will appeal equally to all people. Segmentation allows the product to be presented to significant numbers of people in ways which are relevant to them. Segmentation of the market would, of course, normally be uneconomic for the education service if the segments consisted of people in very small numbers (although such techniques as individual

study programmes can be said to provide a means of adapting a standard product to focus on a market segment of a single student). Effective segmentation allows the market to be approached in ways that are meaningful in terms of the 4 'Ps' and the 6 'Os'. It also entails the identification of market segments which are poorly represented amongst an organisation's customers, some of whom may viably be attracted by a different marketing mix. The factors chosen to distinguish the segments need to be relevant to the operation. In education, age, sex and occupation are likely to be relevant: factors such as hair colour will not be. Illustration 4 gives a simplified indication of how any market of individual consumers may be subdivided, or segmented, according to different characteristics.

Staffing for marketing is complex in some firms which have a chief marketing manager, product group managers and brand managers. It can be simple in others. Whether complex or simple, any organisation has to allocate marketing responsibilities and decide on the best structure to facilitate this allocation.

This need poses questions about staff training and development as well as about the organisational structure of the college. Whilst some colleges have created specific posts carrying marketing responsibilities, few institutions have adopted the procedure of commercial organisations, most of which devote as sizeable resources to marketing as to production or other functions.

In recent years marketing theorists have studied **social marketing**. As a concept it has been introduced by marketing theorists to describe:

'the design, implementation and control of programs seeking to increase the acceptability of a social idea, cause or practice in a target group(s)'. (P. Kotler).

Pressure groups have been studied as organisations which harness marketing techniques to raise public awareness and enlist support for their objectives. Promoting the image of education in general and of FHE in particular, and convincing the whole community of its relevance to many aspects of our social and economic life, requires colleges, LEA's and the government to engage in the social marketing of the service.

Applying the concepts

The application to FHE of the apparently simple concepts of marketing is not easy. Like the social services generally, further education is essentially non-profit making. Nonetheless, the markets for every product and service have their unique features, and many organisations in the public and private sector have to develop marketing policies under constraints which are not always dissimilar and are no less pressing. The particular characteristics of further education which must influence the application of marketing concepts are set out below.

- **Multiple publics**: colleges must work with both 'clients' and 'funders' and these two groups can be further sub-divided into students, their parents, employers, professional bodies, the MSC, LEAs, and so on. The latter occupy a particularly ambiguous position in that they are both the providers of FE and major customers, in the sense that they determine, on behalf of the local community, how much and what type of FE will be offered. It is clearly important that colleges should identify the relative influence of their different 'publics' on the demand for a particular course, prior to making decisions on the strength and direction of their marketing effort.

- **Diversified control of the service provided**: the nature of the courses offered by a college is usually the result of the interplay of a number of semi-autonomous organisations, who do not necessarily work closely together in planning the end-product. Examining boards, approving and validating bodies and MSC determine the basic aims and objectives of many courses; the LEA sets the overall level of resources and, sometimes, the 'mission' of the institution; the college is the determining factor in the detailed allocation of resources between courses and in the quality of the implementation of courses. Colleges are thus constrained in their marketing capabilities in that they do not have full control over the development of some new services (courses) or in the maintenance of existing ones.

- **Multiple objectives**: compared with some business enterprises, FE institutions tend to have a larger range of objectives, most of which are not easily reduced to clear targets expressed in financial terms. Different members of staff will have significantly different perceptions of the college's role, which in turn may clash with the objectives of the LEA and/or certain examining and validating bodies. Key objectives are likely to be related to the 'quality' of the education provided. These may well be defined in vague terms which make it difficult to measure progress towards their achievement. Providers of education and their customers may also have very different views as to what constitutes quality. These factors in turn make it more difficult to develop feasible marketing plans, to monitor their implementation and to demonstrate their value.

- **Who are the competitors?**: FE colleges compete with other educational institutions for scarce resources and for students. However, an aggressive marketing stance, say towards nearby schools, must be considered carefully as it might prove damaging to the image of education in general and to the standing of the college in the local community. It may be as fruitful for FE colleges to conceive of competition in terms of alternative ways for the community's resources to be allocated and for students to spend their time. Such alternatives increasingly include training courses mounted by industrial, commercial and government sponsored organisations.

- **Wants and needs**: Colleges' objectives are often expressed in terms of a response to the perceived needs of the community. But such needs may differ significantly from 'wants' expressed in the recruitment and day release policies of local employers, and in the enrolment of students. It is particularly difficult to introduce a course leading to a new qualification — irrespective of its quality — in any area where there are existing long-established qualifications. The market for FE combines 'consumer' and 'industrial' elements: a mass market of student consumers, and relatively fewer employers whose recruitment and training policies can nevertheless have a substantial impact on student demand. In both elements of the market, there are areas of high responsiveness to new initiatives, and areas of great inertia. Teaching staff, students and local employers may also have very different criteria for judging 'quality of service'. Again, the 'wants' of teaching staff may be incompatible with consumer 'needs'.

— **Systems constraints**: certain features of the UK educational system may well counteract college objectives and marketing plans which support them. There are financial disincentives to teaching staff (in terms of remuneration and promotion) to re-allocate their efforts towards students of lower ability. Other aspects of the Burnham salary arrangements (e.g. the unit total system) have in practice made some colleges keener to support full-time courses than shorter, more flexible offerings on a part-time or block basis. The timescale for LEA, regional and national approval of certain courses militates against a swift response to newly identified market needs. The fact that FHE in the UK is a national system, locally administered, may mean that some elements of its marketing have to be considered at the DES, MSC or LEA levels, rather than in colleges. Furthermore, the government, LEAs or their agencies may wish to limit the provisions of FHE according to economic and social policies, or sponsor its development for one group in the community rather than another. Arrangements for student finance constitute a further constraint.

— **Public scrutiny and 'non-market' pressures**: the maintained sector of FE is under close public scrutiny in view of its claims on the tax and ratepayer. Colleges are likely to experience frequent political pressures and conflicting demands to serve a 'public interest' which is sometimes vaguely defined or impossible to meet fully. Perceptions of success may, however, be critical both to a college's resource base and its autonomy.

The marketing perspective: An agent for change?

Further education, perhaps more than any other social service, needs to know of and respond to economic and social changes. National and local demographic factors are crucial. Our population is aging and one of the consequences of demographic changes since the war is that the system's erstwhile staple market (the 16-21 year old male cohort) will decline as a proportion of the total population. The changed role of women in society and the appeal to assist the achievement of greater equality of opportunity for women and men through wider and easier access to further education is of fundamental significance to an analysis of its market. So too is the response further education is encouraged to make to the rich variety of ethnic minority groups which now make up our communities. The contemporary emphasis on the continuing education of adults also raises questions about traditional definitions of the market for FHE. The economic changes pose questions about the type of market further education faces, not just in the balance of employed to unemployed in our community but also in the nature of skills required, itself a fast changing element. Indeed, the old debates about education for work or leisure become increasingly more sophisticated as arguments proceed not about whether the orientation should be towards vocational or non-vocational education but about the nature of the two types of education to be provided.

In this uncertain sea of social change, further education is not without advice on how to swim. We have already said that the FE system has some strong, if obscure, external regulators. At local and national level, colleges are having their missions shaped for them. But few colleges have precise missions articulated for them by their LEAs. It is more common for only broad guidance to be given, and it is then for the college's academic board or governing body to compose a mission. Whilst this is of critical importance to the definition of the college's market, those who administer a college more often than not have to infer a mission from the sometimes unrelated decisions of governors and academic boards made over several years. This situation makes it vital that LEAs and governing bodies consider and give guidance on the precise marketing targets to be established by a college and its departments. Colleges need the freedom to be 'entrepreneurial' within the parameters of their operations decided by the LEA.

Clearly, colleges do not possess all the powers necessary to enable them to relate to the market place as commercial organisations. For example, they are not often free to fix price, although the LEA has more freedom in this respect. A decision to alter the site of the college's operations so as to change the place of distribution for some courses may not be possible in every case. A particular product might have a very accessible market in the college's area but be outside the mission laid down for it by the LEA. Whilst there may be many limiting factors, the potency of a marketing perspective as an agent for change in further education should not be ignored.

— Its emphasis on the consumer and discovery of the consumer's needs is a radical force for change extending, as it does, to learning arrangements and not just to curriculum matters. A slogan characterising the Action Plan[2] being introduced in Scotland's FE provision is 'Madam, How Do You Want To Learn?' Here a marketing perspective is illustrated which focuses on a particular, underdeveloped segment and on the 'how' rather than the 'what' of provision.

— The organisation of a college's provision, if it is informed by a marketing perspective, will be held under constant review. The segmentation of the college into departments or other units of organisation may not be sufficiently customer orientated. Equally, it is clear that a marketing perspective affects the work of most staff rather than a few of them. The organisational and staff development consequences of a marketing perspective need close examination.

— For senior college managers and LEA officers, the effects of a marketing perspective are likely to be particularly marked. Integrating marketing with academic policy is no easy task; dealing with press relations, community groups, employers and other individuals requires both time and skill if marketing is to be effective.

— Two of the constraints on the organisation of FE — the grading of courses and other arrangements made by the Burnham Committee, and the conditions of service parameters set by the NJC — require some amendment (or imaginative interpretation) if staffing for marketing is to be achieved. Furthermore, there will need to be a generalised acceptance that engaging in marketing is as important a use of staff expertise and resources as is teaching.

- If students are to be regarded as flow and not stock, as life-long customers rather than a cohort of available clients for a particular period in time, the place of a college in its local and national community, and the surrounding services it offers its clients, may need to change dramatically.

In short, a marketing perspective may be the best way to reach the parts that other outlooks on the nature and purpose of FE cannot reach. However, for this to be successful, colleges need to develop a marketing strategy as an integral part of their overall development plan.

The marketing audit

As we have seen, colleges devote some of their resources to marketing. In some cases this will be based on a clear understanding of the market to which the college seeks to relate. In other cases the markets may be only vaguely identified but resources will be devoted, nevertheless, to some of the processes of marketing: to promotion, to advertising, to public relations and so on. These publicity functions may be approached systematically on a college-wide basis, or may have developed haphazardly, being emphasised in some departments (or even just sections of them) but not in others. Hence, it is not the case that colleges do not market themselves — the question is rather one of how effectively they use the marketing resources which they possess. Clearly, before embarking on any new approaches to marketing a college, or a department, there needs to be an assessment of the current position — its strengths and weaknesses and the opportunities and threats which arise from it.

Such a review can be called a **marketing audit.** Its aim is to achieve an overall perspective of current marketing, of the deployment of staff time in marketing, of the use of other resources, of the techniques and approaches of competitors and of the current state of knowledge about the market. It is easy to pose these questions in a general way. A marketing audit requires a rather more detailed framework, if its results are going to be useful. This can be conceived in four parts. Firstly, it is useful to study the college's or department's **strategic profile.** The strategic profile concerns the kind of business the college believes it is in, how it sees its customers and how it relates to them. It also concerns

how the college, department or section sees itself. Secondly, a great deal can be learnt from studying the college's **external environment** by posing questions about the major political, social, economic, technological and educational developments which may affect the college, department or section's development now or in the future.

A third part of the audit framework is the **resource audit.** This questions the capabilities of staff, buildings, equipment, existing procedures, budgets and the college's management organisation to be effective in marketing. Finally, a marketing audit should produce a summary of the college's **current strategy** not just in terms of the marketing processes but also in terms of the college's other strategies for course production and finance and personnel management.

A marketing audit can be developed from a check-list of questions as indicated in Illustrations 5 a-d below. Illustration 5a provides some questions about business definition, competitive posture and the college's or deparment's self-image which may be helpful in assessing the strategic profile. Illustration 5b raises some questions concerning the external environment under four dimensions: the political, social and economic dimension, the market dimension, the product and technological dimension and the competitive dimension. Illustration 5c concentrates on the resource audit, posing questions about operational resources, financial resources, and management and organisational resources. Illustration 5d raises four general aspects of current strategy – production, marketing, finance and personnel.

The questions and themes raised in these illustrations are by no means exhaustive. Nor is there anything sacrosanct about the particular questions raised – those doing the marketing audit need to decide which areas within the framework should be examined.

The critical feature is that the audit needs to be structured. It may be more or less complex in its structure than the example given in illustrations 5 a-d.

ILLUSTRATION 5

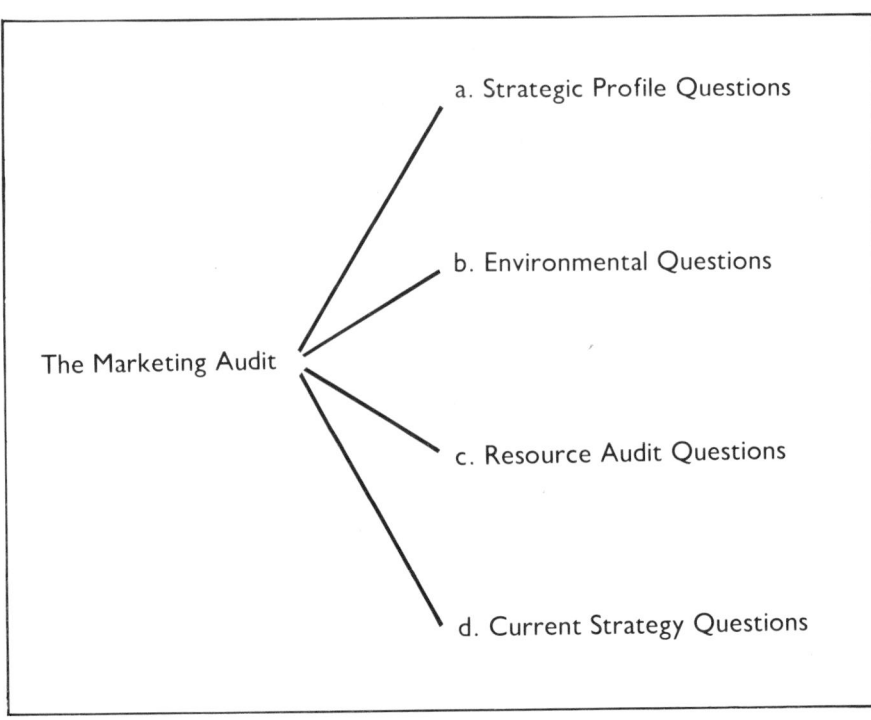

ILLUSTRATION 5 THE MARKETING AUDIT

a. Some Strategic Profile Questions

Business Definition

What is your *product scope* and who are your *target markets?* e.g. vocational education and training for 16-19 year olds in your area, etc.

Mission statement: do you have or can you produce a summary statement of departmental or college objectives or purposes?

Product demand: what kinds of courses and services do your target markets demand or want? e.g. 13 week off the job component of a 12-month work-based scheme.

Functional demand: what functions do your products serve for your customers? e.g. to avoid unemployment, to provide a necessary qualification for career progression, etc.

Generic demand: in the most general sense, what needs do you meet for your customers? e.g. education, leisure/recreation . . .

Vertical integration: to what extent are you formally linked with suppliers of 'raw materials'? (e.g. schools) and consumers of your 'product' (e.g. employers).

Geographic coverage: define your catchment area as precisely as possible.

Competitive Posture

What is your *market position?* Do you have a monopoly; if not, who are your competitors? How big are your target markets and what is your share of them? Are you the market leader in any of your markets?

Which *competitive weapons* do you use? e.g. monopoly power, reputation, exclusiveness, entry qualifications, quality, image, flexibility of response, packaging, brand name (e.g. BTEC), delivery, after-sales service, etc.

College Self Image

Which words would you use to describe the department/college as you and your colleagues see it? e.g. academic excellence, efficient, responsive, flexible, entrepreneurial, aggressive, relaxed, overstretched, threatened, demoralised, confident, weak, strong, bureaucratic, anarchic . . .

ILLUSTRATION 5 THE MARKETING AUDIT

b. Some Environmental Questions

Political, Social and Economic Dimension

What impacts do the following have: rise of MSC, privatisation, student loans, greater central control of local authorities, LEA policy on 16-19 etc?

What impacts do the following have: demographic trends, changes in leisure habits, attitudes towards education and training, increasing numbers of single-parent families, etc?

What impacts do the following have: local industrial context and level of unemployment, impact of regional policies, etc?

Market Dimension

What are the trends in size of your various target markets?

Will the wants and demands of your existing customers change in future?

Which new markets might you exploit, and how big are they? . . .

Product and Technological Dimension

On price, will fees, entry qualifications, cost to employers/sponsors, time taken etc. vary in future? . . .

On life cycles, what is the expected life of present and planned new courses? How is the introduction of new courses to be sequenced? . . .

On new product development, what scope is there for new products to be introduced in your markets? . . .

On resource capacity, what are the major constraints on course and other product development? . . .

Competitive Dimension

Who are the competitors? How easily can new competitors arise to challenge your position? What are the likely future trends? . . .

How will your market share and position change in future?

ILLUSTRATION 5 THE MARKETING AUDIT

c. Some Resource Audit Questions

Operational Resources

On plant, what buildings and equipment are available, what is their actual and potential capacity, on what assumptions? e.g. 48 week year.

On staff, what teachers are available, with what expertise? What are the needs/possibilities for retraining, redeployment, redundancy, new staff? What are the present and likely future levels of non-teaching staff support? . . .

Financial Resources

What is the likely future trend in overall financial provision? Which will be the major sources of funds in future? What are the dominant measures of efficiency (e.g. SSRs, unit costs etc.) and what are the likely future targets? Can you identify areas of waste or slack resources? Can you identify areas which are badly overstretched? . . .

Management and Organisational Resources

Are the present and/or likely future organisation *structures* appropriate to the problems they must solve? What changes are likely? . . .

Are present and/or likely future *procedures* appropriate, e.g. for course management, development and approval, redeployment of resources, etc?

What are the strengths and weaknesses of the people in key managerial positions, now and in the future? What are the strengths and weaknesses of the organisiaton as a whole?

ILLUSTRATION 5 THE MARKETING AUDIT

d. Some Current Strategy Questions

Production Strategy

Which courses will be run, with what modes of attendance, by which groups of staff, where?

What other activities will be undertaken, at what levels of 'output'?

What are the planned stages of development in the department/college offering? . . .

Marketing Strategy

What are your target markets, your orientation to them, the competitive weapons you use, and the marketing mix (product, price, place, promotion) you employ?

How do you see this strategy developing? . . .

Financial Strategy

What are your target SSRs, class sizes, lecturer hours, student hours?

How will you budget for new or replacement equipment, teaching space?

What are your expected future levels of non-teaching staff support and materials/supplies spending? . . .

Personnel Strategy

What is the present and expected future management style in the department/college?

What changes do you expect/will you seek in the teaching staff?

How will organisation structure and procedures change?

What are the likely future trends in salary levels and the academic labour market and how will you respond to them? . . .

The Portfolio ('Boston') Matrix

The Portfolio Matrix is intended to provide a method of identifying the relative success of products, by considering their market share against the size of the market, as indicated in Illustration 6.

ILLUSTRATION 6 THE PORTFOLIO ('BOSTON') MATRIX

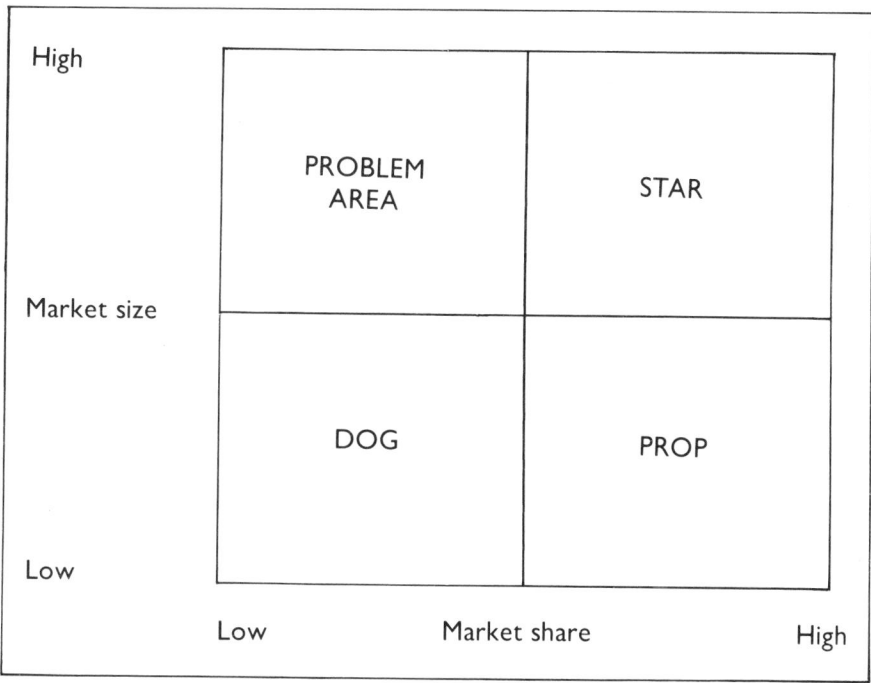

Broadly speaking, the further to the right of the diagram is the product, the less there is to worry about. 'Star' courses will be those which enjoy a large share of a big market (such as secretarial studies or catering). 'Props' are courses which also have a large market share, but of minority markets (such as freight forwarding or mining). 'Problem Areas' exist where courses only enjoy small shares, whilst the real 'Dogs' — areas of provision from which withdrawal should be made if there is no quick and effective way of retrieving the situation — are courses which enjoy a small share of a small market.

The matrix can be, and has been, used as a practical analytical tool as well as a useful conceptual device. There are difficulties, however, in using it with precision in the case of many colleges. This arises principally from the difficulty of obtaining accurate statistics on the size of the market. Many FHE colleges are the sole providers of a particular type of course within their LEA. If market size is taken simply as the total enrolments on this type of course within the LEA, then by definition the college will enjoy a 100% share — clearly a falsely optimistic reading of reality. On the other hand, it may be difficult or impossible to obtain accurate statistics of actual applicants to particular courses within the catchment area of the college.

Despite their limitations, it is still possible to employ the matrix as a means of making valid **internal** comparisons, and of judging relative performance of courses over time. Provided the assumptions made in calculating market size are consistent across the range of college courses (regionally or nationally published statistics may have to be employed) the **relative** position of courses within the institution can be determined. By employing the technique annually, improvements and deteriorations in the position of individual courses can be identified. This can provide a sounder basis for decisions on the long-term future of courses and the resources allocated to them, than 'impressionistic data' and academic hunches. Otherwise it is all too easy to assume that increased enrolments automatically reflect college success, and declining numbers failure. But if market share has moved in the opposite direction the true reading of the position might be rather different. The matrix represents a tool which can help provide a more objective analysis of the position. It can assist in answering questions under the 'competitive posture' section of the marketing audit. A grouping of courses towards the left of the matrix, with a continued trend in that direction, represents a substantial 'threat', and calls for significant action in one or more areas of the marketing 'mix' in order to retrieve the situation.

Summary

Many recent and some longer standing criticisms of FE are directed at its ability to market itself. Whilst some find the idea of marketing education distasteful, the fact is that all colleges employ some marketing approaches even if they have been adopted unconsciously.

The key concepts of marketing are easy to describe but its processes are hard to implement, especially in relation to a social service such as education. However, the marketing approach can be applied in further education and some institutions already employ successful marketing tactics.

The applications of a marketing perspective to the work of a college has a considerable capacity to change many features of its life, including its organisation, the view it adopts of its clients, the activities and training of its staff and the organisation and presentation of its curriculum.

The undertaking of a detailed marketing audit in order to establish the strengths and weaknesses of the college, or department, and the opportunities and threats facing it, is a necessary preliminary to the development of a marketing plan. The portfolio, or 'Boston', matrix is a useful conceptual device for analysing the relative strengths of courses within their overall market.

2. Researching the Market

This section begins by outlining the purpose of **marketing research** as yielding information which assists decision making. As such it is seen to form part of the college's management information system. **Market research** is shown to be just one part of marketing research, involving the studying of samples of the population in order to enable predictions to be made about the characteristics of the population as a whole. It is suggested that considerable benefits can accrue from researching the market. In addition to deciding what information is required and what techniques should be used in any research for further education, it is emphasised that another prior decision will be necessary: by whom should the research be carried out?

The basic **marketing information** which colleges require is outlined as are the **benefits** which can flow from researching the market. **Sources** of this information which can be acquired without survey research are discussed. These include college/student records, government and local authority statistics and the information available from a number of organisations and professional bodies. The range of marketing research, covering **sales research, product research, promotion research** and **export research,** is then outlined before detailed consideration is given to **market-survey research.** Here the advantages, disadvantages, opportunities and difficulties for colleges and LEAs engaging in survey research are outlined. The methods of selecting a **sample** and the main **survey methods** are compared and contrasted and some ground rules on **questionnaire design** are explained. Finally, the need for LEAs and colleges to establish a **market research policy** is discussed.

Marketing research and market research

The purpose of marketing research is to yield information which will assist those who provide further education to make decisions about the provision to be made. As such, marketing research provides information which forms part of a management information system. A management information system is a collection of data which has been selected in order to assist the making of decisions and to effect action. Such a wide definition makes the scope of marketing research virtually unlimited. Resource constraints of time, staff, skill and money mean that FE establishments will need to select appropriate research techniques from the battery of those available to them. A great deal of useful information can be assembled from the desk by a careful exploration of published data, directories and college records. Research need not be costly and a basic profile of the college's immediate market can be achieved and updated with a minimum of effort. Indeed, in contemplating marketing research it is crucial that information is not collected in a random way, or resources

wasted on collecting it at all if decisions can be made without it. Further, the collection of **relevant** information will be more cost effective the easier it is to collect. The marketing information system needs to be easily updated and relevant to the timetable which governs college decision making.

Market research is just one part, albeit the best known, of marketing researching. Market research involves studying facts about or the opinions of (usually) a sample of the population to enable predictions to be made about the characteristics of the population as a whole. Whilst this section deals with the general techniques of marketing research, including market research, it has to be recognised that many colleges will not have the resources to engage in all aspects of market research. Indeed some market research will only be feasible if organised by a consortium of colleges or by the LEA. Certainly, it would be a wasteful duplication of resources for several colleges all to be researching the same markets. Hence, before a college engages in market research a check should be made with the LEA about its own research facilities and plans, and data which has already been recorded.

ILLUSTRATION 7 The Benefits of Researching the Market

Marketing research can help us estimate:
- the extent of the current and potential need for a product
- the size of the total market
- the type and numbers of consumers who might buy the product
- the segmentation of the market
- whether the market is expanding or declining and at what rate
- what share of the market is necessary to make the investment worthwhile
- what are the chances of achieving that share and by when
- how quickly styles or tastes change
- how many competitors there are
- the number and prices of competitive products
- the relative strength of each competitor
- the chances of a new product competing effectively with established ones
- the likelihood of a new product being copied
- the likelihood of new competition appearing
- the chances of our product being able to meet new competition

Researching the Market

Amongst the information which all colleges will need are certain basic facts about the nature of its undifferentiated market. This information can be considered in the following categories:

- basic demographic information: the profile of potential consumers in terms of age, sex, income groups, occupations and social status

- the geographical distribution of potential consumers: a local or national map of relevant population density can be constructed

- the nature of distributive channels e.g. road, bus and train networks to the college; the availability of facilities in the area for off-site working

- the economic and employment profile of the college's area or its labour market intelligence e.g. the changing nature of employment in the area, the degree of training take up by the employers, the regularity and depth of involvement with the college of the employer and his or her current and ex-employees. Similar information will be required concerning the nature and operation of trade unions in the area, and on the level and structure of unemployment

- the range and functions of voluntary organisations and pressure groups within the community

- the market shares of major competitors in the education and training field including other nearby colleges and training centres both public and private

- the availability to potential customers of services which assist their education e.g. crèches, libraries, careers counselling

College records

Much of this kind of information can be assembled from college records, but some will only be achievable by more rigorous information collection from students at the time of their enrolment and graduation. Ideally, the student record should enable a college to know who its past and present students are, where they have come from, how they have got there, why they did so, when they did so and their attitudes to the courses they studied. However, the amount of effort required for this exercise should not be underestimated, and some form of computerised student record is probably needed.

It is equally important to record information on public and private sector employers and schools. The names and addresses of contacts in the company or school, a basic profile of them (e.g. number of employees or pupils on roll), the number and names of employees or pupils sent to the college, are some fundamental categories for maintaining a record of employer-college and school-college links.

Other sources of data

Much of the information required can only be achieved by delving into published and unpublished data sources. Amongst the most useful sources are those listed below:

- the Government's Statistical Service Publications, e.g. Social Trends, reports from the Office of Population Censuses and Surveys, education statistics in DES Bulletins and other publications, the MSC's surveys of employment, the Treasury's Economic Bulletins, the Department of Employment Gazette, the Blue Book of Income and Expenditure, the Annual Abstract and the Monthly Digest of Statistics, evidence to and proceedings of the House of Commons Select Committee on Education and the publications of the National Economic Development Council

- information from Local Authorities' Statistics e.g. the individual authority's surveys of employment and related matters for planning purposes, information collected by the Careers Service, the education estimates of the Chartered Institute of Public Finance and Accountancy, papers of bodies such as the Society of Education Officers

- the reports of professional associations and trade unions e.g. the publications of NATFHE, the APC, ACFHE, the publications of specialist groups, (e.g. the RIC) and teacher groups (e.g. the Business Education Teachers Association), the publications of the Institute of Marketing, especially its World Register of Organisations

- the studies made by academics, such as the Review of the Economy and Employment published by the Institute for Employment Research at Warwick University

- there are many other published sources of information, especially about companies e.g. the Times guide to the top 1000 companies in the UK

- information from competitors such as other colleges and non-college competitors can be a useful source of market information: their prospectuses, annual reports and promotional material provide useful data

- informal networks of colleagues in FE, schools and local government can usually be tapped for those elusive pieces of data

- the MSC's labour market intelligence unit and the Commission's regional officers can provide very detailed data concerning employment and training arrangements in particular areas

- the DES PICKUP (Professional, Commercial and Industrial Updating Project) and CELP (College – Employer Links Project) also offer valuable sources of information, advice and practical assistance in establishing effective identification of employment needs

 Jll list of reference material and the data sources set out above, together with contact addresses, is set out in Section 5. The establishment of a computerised database can assist colleges to store and retrieve easily the large volume of data which can be acquired from the sources dealt with in this section. Indeed, the amount of potentially relevant information involved probably makes necessary the use of a computerised database.

Sales Research

Another fundamental type of marketing research is sales research. A market orientated company will keep a record of the success or failure of different sales methods and the deployment of sales staff. The data required as an aid to judging the effectiveness of different sales approaches in FHE include the following:

- information concerning the territorial variation in course take up.

This should relate to the demographic and other features of the undifferentiated global market

- data concerning sales territories, e.g. the organisation of careers counselling and any revisions in it

- data concerning the effectiveness of different sales methods and people (or departments), e.g. how successful are careers conventions, open days, direct mailing, exhibitions, industrial links, school links, etc., as aids to recruitment

- a record of the resource costs and effectiveness of different forms of distribution, e.g. in-college, on-site, in-company, out-reach, etc.

- the cost of different advertising media, and details of their relative effectiveness in recruiting students

Product Research

Product research and some of its techniques offer low-cost development opportunities for further education. This research involves the analysis of the competitive strength and weakness of existing provision, both of one's own and that made by one's competitors: a topic dealt with in detail in Section I. Existing courses may have a number of new and unexplored markets. Often the concept of a new course or provision will need to be tested to see if employers, community groups and potential students will support it. A further stage may involve testing out a particular provision on a pilot basis (e.g. by on-site arrangements) before a full-scale launch.

Product research can lead to variety reduction. Some full-time and part-time courses might be combined without loss of recruitment. More adventurously, the introduction of short modules common to a number of 'courses', such as in Scotland's Action Plan, may maximise recruitment by achieving greater customer convenience.

Promotion Research

Another aspect of marketing research is promotion research. Colleges may wish to experiment with different approaches to course literature, for example, and keep a record of the success generated by the different approaches. Information on designing course literature can be found in Section 4.

There is little point in undertaking the costs of advertising without keeping a record of the relative effectiveness of different advertising approaches. Media, copy and promotions research enables a record to be kept of effectiveness and a discovery made of the appropriate medium of communication for the market segment which is to be approached. A free local newspaper may be read widely by one age or social group and not others. Ideally, a manager responsible for marketing will know of the client profile of different advertising media before he or she reaches for the cheque book. More detail of the sources of information which assist these judgments can be found in the section on 'Advertising'.

'Export' Marketing Research

For institutions involved in advanced level work in particular, provision of further education for the overseas market 'export' marketing research is an important aspect of their operations. The same research approaches can be applied to this market as are generally described in this section but, of course, the costs involved will be greater.

The research needs are far greater when marketing education in overseas contexts. A wide range of information is needed in preparation long before anyone goes out from the institution being marketed. The information base can be categorised under four headings:
- demographic
- educational
- out-of-country demand and provision
- social, political and cultural background

The basic demographic information includes the same type of statistics as for the UK market, although their breakdown may be substantially different in the context of overseas markets.

Information is also needed on the local education system, and in particular, on its compatibility with the British education systems. Of particular concern are the status of English language teaching, and the acceptability and equivalence of local educational qualifications by British institutions and validating bodies.

The third information category concerns the demand for, and provision of, out-of-country education. This should include details of student placement through bilateral agreements and through the work of the international agencies such as the United Nations agencies. It should also include information on government policies for meeting the demand for education from out-of-country sources, and the extent to which Britain and other providing countries are currently meeting those demands. Information on the reputation of Britain and its educational institutions and on the administrative structure and regulations governing study in the UK should be included here. Information on the kinds of provision made by British institutions and by Britain's major overseas competitors is needed, in as much detail as can be obtained.

The final category of information needs includes relevant and up-to-date knowledge about the country's religious, political, cultural and economic background. In this way the risks of a marketing drive being damaged by social and cultural gaffes can be minimised; and the particular needs of specific groups of overseas students can be identified beforehand. Ways in which the institution plans to meet local requirements can then be used as part of the marketing process.

It may well be beyond the resources of a single institution to acquire a satisfactory information base before designing its marketing strategy. It may, however, be possible to seek help from other institutions with experience in this field. These could be other educational institutions, or commercial organisations — who are likely to co-operate only if the benefits from so doing can be demonstrated as being mutual. Several British government departments have an interest in links between British and overseas educational organisations, including the Department of Education and Science, the Department of Trade and Industry, the Overseas Development Administration and the Foreign and Common-wealth Office. The British Council is particularly important in co-ordinating demand for and provision of educational services to overseas countries. Its country by country series of Higher Education Market Surveys is available to contributory British institutions, and provides a valuable source of information and of suggestions as to appropriate marketing strategies.

Overseas students already studying in this country provide another valuable – but often overlooked – source of information. Not only can they provide details not otherwise available about demand for educational services in their country and strategies for reaching the potential student market: they might also be able to facilitate the institution's marketing activities on their return home, by providing contacts, or even acting as local agents. A survey of overseas students on a country-by-country basis is also important in identifying client perceptions of the institution, the social and cultural milieu in which they are living, and of obstacles which might deter future students from coming to the institution.

Market-survey research

Finally, we come to the most cost-intensive area of marketing research: market-survey research. Whilst cost-intensive, market-survey research has a useful surrogate function: it is a very useful form of advertisement. Indeed, a major benefit of asking employers, and other individuals, their opinions or facts about themselves or their employees is that the asking not only demonstrates an interest in them but also presents them with the existence of the college and, hopefully, the quality of its image. It is possible to reduce costs by doing a pilot survey. This allows decisions to be made about the feasibility of the study, the reliability of the methods adopted, the quality of any questionnaire used, and so on. It is also possible to reduce costs by seeking help from students undertaking training in management, marketing and business studies.

Virtually all social, political and market-survey research proceeds by using a sample of the population to be studied as a proxy for the population itself. Clearly, the smaller the sample the greater the possibility of error, but this possibility can be reduced by accuracy in the selection of the sample and the research approach made to it. To cover the total population in any survey would be prohibitive because of cost, time and administrative complexity except, for example, in the case of the ten-yearly census.

Selecting a sample

A sample can be selected by either a random or a quota method. In random sampling all elements in the population have an equal chance of selection. In quota sampling the population is split into categories and the categories are themselves randomly selected to produce the overall sample. Quota sampling is cheaper than random sampling and easier to administer. However, its use increases the probability of error. Many educational surveys have used quota sampling. For example, the

Robbins Report was based on a sample of LEAs, the choice of schools within the selected LEAs and eventually the selection of individuals within the schools. The use of smaller and smaller categories to produce a sample is known as multi-stage sampling.

Quota sampling operates on the basis of pre-designed controls on the population. Interviewers are assigned a profile of the population and the numbers to be included in the survey from each element in the profile, e.g. x women in the 30-39 age group. The interviewers select the respondents to fill those categories. This method is used widely in audience and public opinion research.

Longitudinal or panel surveys allow the measurement of change (e.g. in opinion) over time. The Douglas studies of child progress were based on a panel of children. This approach would allow the testing of the effect of an attempt to change the college's image.

It is a well-established notion in survey research that the quality of the sampling frame (i.e. the list of the population from which the sample is taken) will affect the accuracy of the results produced. Clearly if some items are missing from the frame they have no chance of being included in the sample. An error in the method of selection of the sample or a high non-response rate can also cast doubt on the results of the investigation.

The sampling method and the frame used should relate to the purposes of any study. For example, a survey of training achievements and needs of the employed might well use firms as a stage in the achievement of the sample. An attempt to gauge the way the college is viewed by the population of young people generally might use schools and then registers as a means of selection.

The survey method

Equally important in survey work is the survey method to be applied to the sample. Essentially there are three types of survey method: mail surveys, telephone surveys and personal (interviewed) surveys. They vary in their relative costs, accuracy and level of non-response, as well as by other factors.

Personal interviewing allows interviewer bias but gives good response and one which is spontaneous. Telephone interviews entail relatively low cost but relate only to those who have a telephone. Postal questionnaires avoid interviewer bias but are impersonal. Mail surveys also have a high non-response rate which itself can be reduced by the inclusion of a stamped addressed envelope (which is essential), brevity and a polite covering letter explaining the purposes of the research.

Questionnaire design is not a simple matter. Some ground rules are set out below.

- Every question should be clear and, if possible, require a 'yes' or 'no' answer (i.e. dichotomous). In certain circumstances, however, it will be necessary to include multiple choice or open-ended questions.

- Leading questions should be avoided.

- The questions should be arranged logically and in a language under-stood by those being consulted.

- Questions should be short, simple and restricted to the respondent's own experience. They should cover one point at a time.

- The layout of the questionnaire should allow easy coding of the

ILLUSTRATION 8 The Survey Methods Compared

Survey Method − Selection criteria

Complexity of questionnaire
Amount of data required
Desired accuracy
Control of sample
Interview control
Time available
Acceptable level of non-response
Cost

	Strengths of the 3 survey methods		
	MAIL	TELEPHONE	PERSONAL
Complexity	Poor	Good	Excellent
Amount	Fair	Good	Excellent
Accuracy	Good	Fair	Fair
Control	Fair	Good	Excellent
Interview Control	Excellent	Fair	Poor
Time	Poor	Excellent	Fair
Level of Non-response	Fair	Fair	Fair
Cost	Good	Good	Poor

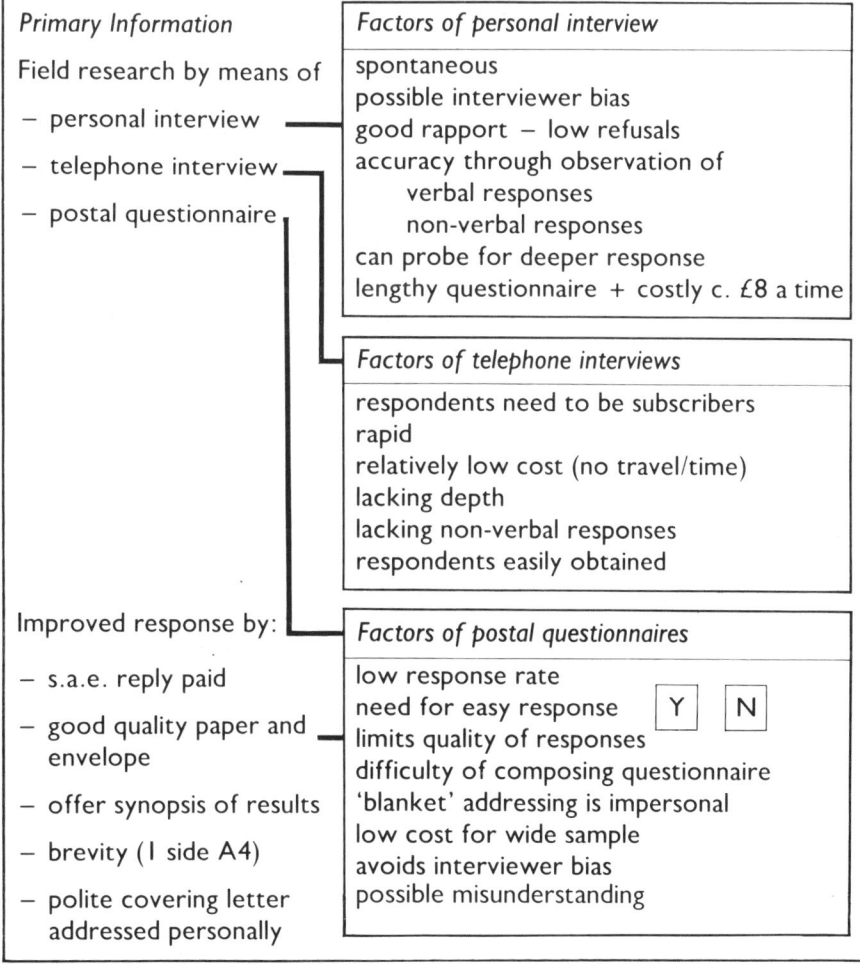

Primary Information

Field research by means of

− personal interview

− telephone interview

− postal questionnaire

Factors of personal interview

spontaneous
possible interviewer bias
good rapport − low refusals
accuracy through observation of
    verbal responses
    non-verbal responses
can probe for deeper response
lengthy questionnaire + costly c. £8 a time

Factors of telephone interviews

respondents need to be subscribers
rapid
relatively low cost (no travel/time)
lacking depth
lacking non-verbal responses
respondents easily obtained

Improved response by:

− s.a.e. reply paid

− good quality paper and envelope

− offer synopsis of results

− brevity (1 side A4)

− polite covering letter addressed personally

Factors of postal questionnaires

low response rate
need for easy response   Y   N
limits quality of responses
difficulty of composing questionnaire
'blanket' addressing is impersonal
low cost for wide sample
avoids interviewer bias
possible misunderstanding

(From Cawthray, B. Putting it Together 5. Marketing & Advertising. South West Regional Management Centre. 1982)

returns. This will be especially important if the data collected is to be analysed by computer.

In deciding on the particular research approach to be adopted, the first step to be taken is the definition of the problem which requires investigation. The next step is to specify the approximate value of the information which will emerge.

Following that, the method of data collection, the techniques of measurement to be used and the sample to be surveyed can be selected. Finally, in deciding on the feasibility of the exercise, an estimate of the time and cost involved will be necessary.

Piloting the questionnaire with a small number of respondents can assist in making judgements about the feasibility of the exercise. Piloting can indicate whether or not the questions have been framed well, are in the best order, are understandable, lead to bias, need supplementing and so on.

Marketing research policy

There is a need for the LEA and the college or polytechnic to devise a marketing research policy. This should deal with the level at which research will be undertaken by the LEA and the college respectively. The target population — employers or individuals — will need to be decided in each case. A budget to cover research costs will be necessary. Above all, the policy should allow the determination of when 'desk' and 'field' research are needed and on what occasions survey techniques are required. The aim of research is to assist decision making; the collection of information is a means to this end, not an end in itself.

Summary

Marketing research is to be distinguished from market research which is one of its parts. Other aspects of marketing research involve sales, product, advertising and export research. Marketing research can make a useful contribution to the college's information system by providing data about the existing and potential market for a particular provision and the competition it faces or may come to face.

Much marketing research is not costly and can be done 'off the desk' by an examination of college records, official and other statistics, and existing arrangements for 'selling' the provision, developing and advertising it.

Market-survey research is cost intensive and requires expertise in the selection of a sample, choosing and applying the survey method to be used and in the design of any questionnaire which might be utilised. However, its application will be feasible in certain cases and, if used sensibly, it has the hidden advantage of promoting the college to those who are surveyed.

3. Organising for marketing – Products, delivery and pricing

Synopsis

This section is concerned with three of the four p's of marketing – product, place (i.e. delivery) and price – and the implications of marketing for college organisational structures.

The need for an effective **product strategy** is dealt with first, and related to the concept of the product life cycle. It is pointed out that colleges have a substantial influence over **product quality** even though product design decisions are often taken centrally by examining and validating bodies. Effective product strategies depend on a clear **identification of the market** and its needs, which courses can then be designed to satisfy. Examples are given of how some colleges have followed this approach with success. Some features of the changing needs of the FHE market are then outlined, and it is emphasised that **the customer's perception** of the product is the one which matters most. The need for continued review and adjustment of the **product range** is discussed, together with the **constraints** on the development of entirely 'custom built' products. The moves towards **customer-centred curricula** are then analysed in terms of their contribution towards an effective product strategy. The problems of **new product development** are outlined and related to the benefits of effective marketing research. An examination of the importance of the relationship between **staffing** and **other resources**, and product quality follows, and the consideration of the products of the FHE service concludes with a look at outlets in overseas markets.

The consideration of the **delivery** of the products of FHE to its customers commences with an investigation of the many **restrictions on access** to educational services – in the form of entry qualifications, age barriers, geography, 'seasonal' availability, attendance requirements and limitations on choice of studies. **Ways of improving access** are then outlined which can match costs and benefits to achieve viable delivery systems – including recent developments in customer-centred delivery, adjustments to the traditional college year, flexible delivery for employers, and open learning.

Pricing is then examined. It is stressed initially that there are increasing **opportunities** for colleges to have a significant influence on pricing policy, even though there are still many **constraints** on their freedom of action. The various elements which constitute the 'price' of the FHE product are then looked at from the **viewpoint of the potential customer**. This leads to a consideration of pricing policy as a **customer-derived** activity, with key pricing policy questions being identified. Cost recovery cannot be ignored, however. **Costing classifications** are therefore discussed as a preliminary to examining the links between **pricing, costing and**

corporate objectives. The key **costing policy questions** are also identified.

The section concludes by discussing marketing in relation to **college organisation**. The drawbacks of a **product-centred** (as opposed to a customer-centred) approach are identified. **Two alternative organisational structures** are examined from the viewpoint of their effectiveness in accommodating the marketing function. Positive staff **attitudes** towards marketing are emphasised as a necessary foundation of any effective structure. The need for **flexibility** is also stressed, especially in the co-operation of staff within and between the marketing function and those responsible for the day-to-day provision of a quality product.

The 'products' of further and higher education
Product Strategy

The products of colleges are usually courses, although research and consultancy services also play an important role, particularly in polytechnics and institutes of higher education. An effective 'product strategy' requires decisions on the type and range of courses to be offered and the quality of their implementation. Decisions on the mix of products involve regular attention to the development of new courses, and the withdrawal of those where provision is no longer cost-effective. The concept of the product life cycle (see Illustration 3 in Section 1) suggests that it is dangerous for any organisation to have a product range weighted towards the 'maturity' and 'decline' stages. It should also be remembered that new product development needs to be a constant concern if it is to bring success: it should not be engaged in merely as an ad hoc replacement strategy for declining products.

Product Quality and the College

There is an understandable tendency for the Non-Advanced Further Education (NAFE) sector to view itself as having only limited influence on product strategy decisions. Most courses in NAFE colleges tend to lead to the qualifications of examining, validating or professional bodies and be based on centrally designed course specifications and syllabuses. The college, in effect, has a retail franchise for these 'national' products. Nonetheless, colleges still exercise crucial authority over the particular courses to be offered, and in the allocation and management of human and physical resources which determine the quality of their operation. It has long been accepted that whilst good teaching can alleviate a poor syllabus, the best designed course in the world will not achieve its objectives if the teaching is incompetent. **The college therefore plays a major part in determining product quality as it is perceived by the customer.**

Identifying the Market – the Prerequisite of an Effective Product Strategy

As we have seen, the foundation of a successful strategy is the identification of the market.

> 'Marketing of courses must start from the base line of clear objectives. The College must know which client groups it is expecting to make provision for. Programmes and courses must then be planned to meet the needs of these groups.'
> (Brenda Remington, Principal, Haringey College)

Questions need to be asked and answered about:

— who are the customers?
— what are their needs?
— do we have existing products to meet those needs?
— if so, do they satisfy these needs as well as they could?

— if not, can and should we design new products, or modify existing ones to meet these needs?

Meeting Customer Needs

Some examples can be given of the practical applications of this type of approach. Haringey College, a new FE college established in 1983, had clear objectives laid down for it from the outset by the Local Education Authority in terms of the client groups for whom it was expected to provide. Specifically identified were school-leavers requiring non-advanced level courses who journeyed to colleges in other boroughs, and groups with special needs — the handicapped, the disadvantaged, the unemployed, minority ethnic groups and women — whose take-up of further education was considerably less than the average for the population as a whole. The correct identification of these groups as possessing educational needs which had previously gone unfulfilled led to a provision of courses which have been successful in attracting students up to the capacity of the current accommodation in the college's first year of operation.

At a more specific level, Southgate Technical College has used its system of departmental advisory committees (each of which has up to twelve industrial/commercial members, in addition to college staff and governors) to identify needs for which courses have then been developed.

> 'Through these Committees we have (over the years) evolved many successful short courses . . . varying from the 'Conversion to Colour' course for TV Technicians in 1964-65 when in one summer vacation we dealt with 700 TV installation engineers from one firm alone, through programmes such as 'Abrasive Wheel Regulations' which are still a hardy annual to such up to date efforts as 'Introduction to Micro-processors' and 'Microelectronic Principles' where we find ourselves going to Thorn EMI on a series of in-house courses'.
> (Bill Easton, Principal, Southgate Technical College)

The desire to seek an effective way of utilising the college provision during the Summer vacation was a catalyst which led Nelson and Colne College to investigate local community needs. A Summer School was organised for mentally and physically handicapped children, with the sponsorship of local business. A community need was met, local business was involved, and the media publicity which was created promoted a positive image of the college in the locality.

John Cassels, Director-General of NEDO, has suggested the formation of 'local user groups' by employers, to which the MSC would contribute some underpinning, and in which educationalists and trade union representatives would take part.

Changing Market Needs

Consideration of the product range against the needs of the market is a continuing requirement. It does not apply solely to new colleges, or to expansion into new areas. The demand for education is changing and at an increasingly swift rate. Certain political, social and economic trends are already beginning to have a substantial impact:

— The overall decline in the number of school-leavers who make up a significant proportion of FHE enrolments. Total college enrolments will continue to wane unless participation rates can be improved and new markets attracted.
— The introduction of new technology, especially information technology, which creates a demand for new skills and for combining new and established skills, but which leaves others redundant.

- Changes in the structure of the family and in the role of women in society, which has brought many more women on to the labour market.
- A steady growth in the number of leisure hours in relation to work hours.
- The decline of mass employment in 'heavy' industry, and the growth of 'hi-tech' business, with fewer, but more highly skilled employees. This has already brought about dramatic reductions in the traditionally healthy demand for certain long-established part-time courses. There has also been a shift in the national economy from unskilled to skilled work, from manual to non-manual, and from manufacturing to services.
- Allied to the above, the rise of long-term youth unemployment, which has brought with it an increase in the participation rate for full-time courses and MSC sponsored training schemes, especially amongst the average and below average ability ranges.
- The increasing involvement of MSC in all aspects of work-related further education, which demands a coherently planned response from LEAs and their colleges.
- The increasingly multi-ethnic nature of our society, bringing with it a wide range of different cultural and educational needs.

Seen in the above context, developments such as the introduction of the Youth Training Scheme (YTS) cannot be dismissed as a temporary hiatus in a constant and tranquil pattern of FHE course provision. Product change is also becoming increasingly institutionalised, with regular syllabus changes and reapproval periods imposed by the examining and validating bodies. It is therefore necessary to be alive to courses which have entered the 'decline' phase of their life-cycle. Is the decline terminal? Can the course be updated to cover new skill and product needs and successfully 'relaunched', or otherwise be rejuvenated by, for instance, offering it to a different clientele? If the decline is irreversible then it is in everyone's interests that resources are switched to courses which are more successful at meeting the real needs of the customers.

There is increasing interest in the responsiveness of courses to changing market needs. For example, MSC now offers support for LEA projects in work-related NAFE aimed at identifying market needs and demands more effectively, developing courses and updating staff.

The Customers' View of Your Product

When taking product decisions it should be remembered that courses are perceived differently by the 'buyer' (student, employer, MSC Managing Agent, etc.)[3] and the seller (college/department). Customers need to be convinced that **they** are being given real benefits in exchange for their time and money. The acquisitions of work-related competences and qualifications which allow further career and educational opportunities are clear motivating factors of the customers of vocational courses. The customers of non-vocational courses may have less direct material motivation, but will still look for the benefit of self-satisfaction in learning, the facility to pursue leisure interests, and so on. There are also the product benefits of social contact which are less direct, but nonetheless significant. The less restricted and more 'adult' environment of college may be perceived by some students as the key benefit which persuades them to study a particular course there rather than at school. Recognition of where the customer most perceives benefits is essential to an effective product − for instance, a poor placement rate into employment and/or further education and training at the end of a course may sound its death knell however well its content is taught. One advantage of maintaining contact with college leavers is that records of placement rates can be assembled. A guarantee that a course will not be subject to amendment before its completion may be another way of bolstering its quality in the eyes of the customer. College contact with ex-students in the form of social activities and so on can also be seen as an 'after sales service' which enhances the reputation of its products.

Product Mix

A college's range (or 'mix') of courses and other services needs to be kept under continual review to ensure that it is making the optimum contribution to the achievement of corporate objectives.

The college's 'product mix' can be varied according to factors such as course level, subject area, mode of study, duration and qualification, in order to meet customer needs at the optimum relationship of benefits and costs. It has been pointed out that in some cases these decisions are constrained by the control of central bodies, although considerable local flexibility is often possible within the overall framework of a national qualification. PICKUP[4] style short courses designed to meet specific adult employment needs offer colleges considerable autonomy in course design and implementation.

Constraints

The primacy of customer benefits does not mean that product considerations are neglected. It is clearly more sensible to build on known strengths than to enter areas in which the college is unlikely to have the staff or resources to offer a quality product. There are clear advantages in the economies of scale and division of labour involved in the educational equivalent of mass production − the course which leads to an established national qualification. As with cars or clothing, the custom-designed or tailor-made model geared to the precise needs of an individual consumer is a very expensive (although sometimes viable) option. The design of courses to meet the needs of individual employers will usually involve some trade-off between the extremes of rigid standardisation and 'one-off' production runs. A number of institutions have developed independent study programmes which entail variation of a standard product to meet individual student needs. It is especially important here that the flexibility which is allowed within the standard framework of national qualifications is exploited to the full.

Customer-Centred Curricula

Seen in this light, the move towards 'student-centre' learning is an indication that FHE is becoming more committed to a market-orientated product strategy. It is, in fact, an implicit recognition that students perceive quality more in terms of what they actually learn and how they are enabled to learn than on the basis of teachers' schemes of work. Curriculum development is concerned essentially with the maintenance and improvement of the quality of existing products and the development of new ones. When properly directed it becomes a crucial part of the college's ability to respond to changing needs. Teaching staff can be helped to play a co-ordinated role if relevant curriculum information (for example, examining body guidelines, new syllabuses and news of technological developments in their subject area) is regularly circulated to them, in a summarised form when appropriate. In recent years there has been a greater emphasis on the advantages of establishing an effective team of staff, who work together to plan and implement a course. This again is a welcome reflection of a more customer-centred approach – an attempt to control the quality of the product in the form the student experiences it, rather than as an unrelated set of separate components. A customer-orientated definition of the teachers' role is that of creating and managing effective learning opportunities for the student.

Acceptance of student-centred approaches does not mean a slavish adherence to the maxim 'the customer is always right'. Counselling and guidance to students and advice to employers are integral parts of the FHE product. Concepts such as the negotiated curriculum (a feature of the new Certificate in Pre-Vocational Education) are aimed simply at taking more account of the customer's wishes, by making a course more adaptable to individual requirements. Equally, a college's probity in advising students from the viewpoint of their own interests can be a long-term product strength. Counselling which results in non-enrolment on a particular course is not necessarily a failure – it can add far more to the reputation of the college than attracting students to courses with promises which are ultimately unfulfilled.

New Product Development

The development of a new product tends to be expensive and time-consuming, whatever type of organisation is involved. Indeed, in industry it is common for the Research and Development function to investigate actively a very large number of ideas for each 'winner' which eventually emerges. Once again effective market research will help to minimise the risk of committing resources to a new course which does not in practice attract sufficient students. The successful launch of a course will often require effective liaison with other organisations. LEAs, RACs, the MSC and examining and validating bodies all have their course approval procedures. A well presented submission document, based on hard evidence of need for the new course, is therefore an essential element of new product development in FHE.

In addition to investigating market need and competition, effective new product development requires that consideration is given to a number of other fundamental questions:

- How efficiently can the new course be operated?
- How will the course be staffed and otherwise resourced? What staff development activities are required? If new staff and/or resources are necessary, how will they be obtained and integrated with those which are already utilised?
- Will there be problems with the non-availability of certain kinds of

expertise and supporting resources?
- What are the likely costs of operation in total and unit costs?
- What are the implications of the course for student-staff ratios, class sizes, student hours and staff conditions of service?
- What returns will accrue to the college and/or LEA from the operation of the course, how will they be assessed and what costs will they be set against?

The development of new products in education is subject to diversified control, as pointed out in Section 1. It is clearly essential for there to be effective liaison between the DES, MSC, examining and validating bodies, LEA's and the colleges, if confusion in strategy and wasteful duplication of effort are to be avoided.

Product Quality and Staffing

Most of us involved in education would accept that the staffing of a course is the most important influence on its quality. Although this is to some extent a reflection of a teacher-centred view of the product, it is clear that this is the point at which the college has greatest control.

'Effective marketing depends on the attitude of the **entire** staff of a college. The marketing function cannot be the sole perogative of a Vice-Principal or Head of Department. A commitment to the 'customers' needs to be looked for when a new member of staff is interviewed. And the college management must at all times provide leadership and project a positive image of the college to the other staff'.
(David Moore, Principal, Nelson & Colne College.)

The type of staff selected and allocated to a course can be influential on its quality as perceived by particular market segments.

'We have established particularly good relationships with this group (The Women's Education and Training Project) in that they have assisted us in finding female lecturers for computing and basic carpentry. This enabled us to have successful role models when we were trying to attract women onto courses where men traditionally predominate.'
(Brenda Remington, Principal, Haringey College).

Recruitment, training and development of college staff can clearly make an important contribution to product quality. In particular, staff need to understand student-centred methods of learning and assessment. Keeping up to date with the impact of changing technology is also of obvious importance in the case of vocational courses. Computer literacy for all teaching staff within the near future has been suggested as vital if the customer perception of the FHE product range is not to be one of increasing obsolescence. This has major implications for the allocation of staff time, as does the continuous need to plan and evaluate courses.

If a college's product mix is to adjust continuously to changing market needs, staff must clearly be very adaptable in their ability to absorb new teaching methods, to update their existing subject knowledge and gain competence in new subjects. All this is unlikely to be achieved without a coherent policy for development, retraining and redeployment, backed by adequate resources. Effective learning strategies are an essential element of successful marketing in education. Monitoring of product quality therefore demands some evaluation of effectiveness so far as the customers are concerned. Hence one of the ways in which a college's marketing strategy relates to its overall strategies is in the areas of course evaluation and staff appraisal and development.

Other Resources and Product Quality

Resources other than staff also help to determine course quality. Many vocational courses require complex and sophisticated equipment to keep pace with employer needs. In some areas it may become too expensive for all but a handful of colleges to continue to meet needs for highly specific skills, unless the employer's own equipment and premises can be used. In other cases effective compromises may be possible (for example, teaching word processing on general purpose micros rather than on 'dedicated' machines). At a more basic level, a favourable attitude to a course amongst students can be sustained by having sufficient library resources to support the work which is set. The standard of accommodation is a particularly important feature of the product if senior staff from industry and commerce are to be attracted. It is often this aspect, as much as the quality of content, teaching and equipment, which causes this segment of the market to turn to private sector providers.

Teachers and the resources which support them are not the only significant influences on the quality of a course. Administration of student admissions, queries, results and periodic reports to employers are also part of the product as perceived by the customer. Inefficiency in these areas creates discontent and throws doubt on quality in other areas. Regular liaison with employers and other agencies who are major customers of the college is a vital element in the overall service which is expected. The initial administrative responses to those attracted by a college's marketing and recruitment strategies are of particular importance in shaping their perception of the product under consideration.

Overseas Markets

It is only recently that the marketing of UK further and higher education in overseas markets has begun to be taken seriously by institutions and government organisations. The main stimulus has probably been the serious losses inflicted upon many institutions by the government's decision to demand full cost fees from overseas students, at a time when international competition for overseas students was increasing. As increasingly rigid ceilings have been applied to UK student numbers in many areas of advanced further education, overseas students have offered one of the few remaining areas for possible expansion. Institutions are coming to realise, however, that such expansion can only be achieved by a sensibly conceived, properly planned and adequately resourced marketing policy.

Emphasis has been given in Section 2 of the handbook to the marketing research necessary before designing a market strategy for overseas markets. The costs involved in overseas marketing are likely to be greater in relation to potential returns than are the costs of UK-based marketing strategies. It is only when as much information as possible has been acquired and analysed that decisions should be made concerning whether or not a marketing approach in a particular overseas country or institution is worth initiating or continuing. If the decision here is affirmative, the specific strategy and tactics can then be prepared — again on the basis of information collected. The marketing strategy should be properly costed. It may be the case that a single institution cannot afford to invest resources on the scale required. However, a collaborative venture between several institutions may be feasible. Recently British universities and polytechnics have co-operated in marketing their facilities and expertise on a regional basis. It might also be possible to collaborate with commercial organisations with compatible interests. In designing specific strategies, the points made elsewhere in the handbook on organising for marketing and the marketing processes are also relevant to overseas marketing, with the obvious proviso that they must take account of local conditions — and that social and cultural mores may well differ sharply not only between countries but even within countries. Tactics successful in one context may therefore be inappropriate in another.

Marketing abroad need not just be concerned with attracting overseas students to UK institutions. Other services should not be overlooked. Consultancy and in-country training may well be more marketable than UK-based further and higher education. It is only through a comprehensive and regularly up-dated information base that client needs can be identified and monitored.

Delivering the product — The right place at the right time

'Q. When is a refrigerator not a refrigerator?
A. When the fridge is in Newcastle and the customer is in Bristol'
(Anon.)

'If we have meals-on-wheels, mass x-ray-on-wheels, libraries-on-wheels, why can we not have education services-on-wheels? Let us

take education to where the customer is, not simply rely on the customer coming to our hallowed halls'.
(Wills, Prof. G. *Marketing of Educational Services* (unpublished paper) June 1973).

Delivery — Restrictions on Access

Traditionally, it has been expected that education will be sought out by the customer at the times and places it was available. Against this, it can be argued that further education has been more influenced by customer requirements than other sectors of the UK education system. The provision of evening courses is but one example which clearly reflects a timing which is convenient to many potential students (or employers), rather than any administrative convenience. It also has to be recognised that other sectors of education are beginning to modify their provision in response to changing social and employment requirements. Nonetheless, most FHE courses are still constrained in their availability to the customer by restrictions on entry, age, physical location, starting date, duration, choice of studies and so on. All of this means that some potential customers may fail to take up a product in which they would otherwise be interested. Some of the most significant restrictions are indicated in detail below.

- Entry qualification restrictions[5]: Many FHE courses cannot be undertaken unless certain specific educational qualifications have already been obtained. This practice is usually a reflection of the imposition of minimum course entry requirements by examining and validating bodies, and of a rationing process carried out by individual colleges when demand for a course outstrips the number of places which are available. It can be defended as a device which helps protect the 'quality' of a course, and which assists in preventing the customer from making inappropriate choices. Criticism is growing, however, that barriers to entry and progression in FHE are over-restrictive and that in practice they stifle potential and kill motivation. It is certainly worth noting that CSEs, GCEs and degrees (in their OU guise) can all, in theory, be obtained by students who are denied the opportunity to enter for some of the qualifications common in FHE. There is also evidence to suggest that possession of particular educational qualifications is by no means as efficient a predictor of future achievement as the use of these restrictions in practice would appear to suppose. Qualification restrictions reflect a view of progress in education as a climb up the ladder of increasing academic rigour. Such a view inevitably excludes a larger proportion of the population at each stage. It is increasingly being argued that many people have a continuing need for learning, the satisfaction of which does not imply their achievement of higher planes of intellectual achievement, and that they have just as much right to be included within any notion of educational progression.

- Age restrictions[5]: The starting point for further education is defined by the sixteen year minimum age for the termination of compulsory secondary education. Age then becomes closely linked with qualification restrictions in the hierarchical nature of educational progression. Age restrictions can be defended for reasons similar to those which are put forward in favour of qualification barriers. Age alone is unlikely to be a very precise indicator of the academic ability which is necessary to gain benefit from a particular course, although it may be a better reflection of social maturity. Nonetheless, the marketing task of FHE is made more difficult by the fact that many of our young people understandably believe that an educational summit has been reached at the age of sixteen and that there is little point in proceeding further.

- Geographical restrictions: The location of colleges on one or several sites is usually an accident of history or politics, and rarely a decision inspired by marketing considerations. Colleges do expand in areas where there is a demand for their provision, but a shift in demand will not often be followed by a shift of the college premises. In general, the further the course is located from potential customers, the more reluctant they will be to avail themselves of it. This is a matter of personal inconvenience as well as cost and time. In areas where public transport is poor or non-existent it may be physically impossible for non-car owners to gain access to most educational 'products'.

- Seasonal restrictions: Many of FHE's products are seasonal in the sense that they can only be 'purchased' at a particular time of year. The September starting date of most traditional FHE courses fits in well with the requirements of recent school-leavers, but is highly restrictive for many other potential customers. Interest in and desire for a course may be aroused in December: there is a good chance that it will have faded if it cannot be translated into actual participation until nine months later. The parcelling of courses to fit the 'straightjacket' of academic terms can also deter customers.

– Attendance requirement restrictions: The regularity of attendance required by most courses will also exclude some potential customers. Shift workers, people whose job involves travel away from home and single parents are just some of those who may find it impossible to come to college at the same time each week or to attend at all. In practice it is often impossible to undertake a course by means of a variable attendance pattern, and/or to extend it over a longer chronological period. Some people may be able and willing to commit themselves to a specific number of hours at a time when the college is open, but all available courses in the area concerned may require a longer period to complete. There is often little possibility of students progressing at their own pace, dependent on their own potential and convenience: most courses have standardised starting and completion dates.

– Study choice restrictions[5]: Resource considerations inevitably place a limit on the different studies which a student might undertake and the ways in which they can be combined. Further limitations on choice may then be imposed by course designers, both at national level and within individual colleges. These are usually intended to produce a better quality product from the viewpoint of coherence, relevance and the prevention of choices which could harm the longer-term interests of the students. The recent growth of 'grouped courses' and 'cores' of study reflects these intentions, but also raises the question of the degree to which any restriction on freedom of choice deters some potential students from enrolling.

Improving Access: Matching Costs and Benefits

Once again, effective marketing requires that trade-offs are made between costs and customer benefits. In the same way as most people choose to go to their local supermarket to buy food, rather than paying extra to have it delivered to their door, it will not be viable to provide a custom-designed course at the home of each individual student. Nonetheless, considerable flexibility can be built into the standard course provision to co-ordinate it better with the varied requirements of potential students. It is also important to note that effective marketing segmentation does not require the imposition of restrictions on access, even though a course may be aimed at a very specific group of students.

Some techniques for dealing with problems of access are considered below:

– Developments in customer-centred delivery systems: A number of recent developments in FHE represent an implicit recognition that more customer-centred delivery systems are needed if new markets are to be attracted, and if existing customers are not to be lost in increasing numbers to private sector providers. MSC's New Training Initiative (NTI) places great emphasis on opening up access and reducing barriers to training. The Open-Tech Scheme is offering opportunities to learn and qualify with many of the traditional restrictions on access removed. The moves towards the modularisation of some courses are aimed at maximising the choices open to students within the framework of a standard 'menu'. The Scottish 'Action Plan', for instance, is based on a comprehensive framework of 40 hour modules which allows for a very high degree of freedom in selection of studies. Many grouped course schemes in the rest of the UK have built up flexible arrangements for 'optional' or 'additional' studies which can be combined with the compulsory core. At the local level a number of colleges have themselves established open learning opportunities. Nelson and Colne College recently opened DISC – the Drop-In Skills Centre–to provide open-access learning in technical skills at the convenience of the customer. Haringey College has a multi-skills workshop which operates on similar lines. Courses mounted in co-operation between two or more colleges also provide a means of widening access to the same choice of products. Credit transfer systems can open up more opportunities for progression by recognising the validity of previous learning gained elsewhere.

– The college year: Some colleges have extended their period of opening to occupy the full calendar year rather than the traditional 'academic year'. Alternative course starting dates have been offered and, in conjunction with the central bodies concerned, examinations can be taken on demand rather than at one or two set times. Much of the pressure for this has come from the increased involvement of FHE in MSC-sponsored training schemes. In relation to FHE, the MSC is, in fact, not only a partner in vocational training but also an actual and potential customer with major spending power and an inclination to shop around for the best buy – outside the maintained sector if it cannot meet the required specification, which includes a heavy emphasis on flexible availability. Whatever the catalyst, the effect has been to cause some colleges to re-examine their delivery methods across their whole range of provision and not just in the area of publicly funded off-the-job training. Qualifications may be offered via a variety of study modes. Students may be allowed to accumulate credits and eventually qualify in a timescale which is more convenient to them. These are all means of extending the appeal of the same basic product.

– Flexible delivery and employers: Flexible delivery is an important selling point of vocational courses, even though part-time students may be committed to attend a course as a condition of their employment. An employer is seeking an educated and trained workforce. The college has the expertise to educate and to train. Such expertise need not be dependent on a particular physical location. Employers may be happier to 'buy in' college expertise and have it applied on in-house training premises. A number of PICKUP initiatives are of this nature. (The same arguments apply to college delivery of its services on the premises of other educational institutions, such as schools).

– Open learning and expanding the market: Open learning systems can be classified under three main headings:

college-based: here students attend college but are able to study at a time and pace of their own choice – as, for example, in the 'learning by appointment' centres at St. Albans, Bath and Napier colleges;

local: most students live within easy travelling distance of college but spend most of their study time at home – learning is based on a written 'package' and the college provides counselling, tutorial and assessment services. These 'flexistudy' arrangements were pioneered at Barnet College in 1977 and have since been adopted extensively elsewhere;

distant: students pursue correspondence courses, which are sometimes supplemented by counselling and include periods of residential study, as in the case of the SCOTBEC awards for people living the in the Highlands and Islands, remote from any college.

Open learning is sometimes seen as a 'low-cost' alternative. This is a mistaken view. Although there is a reduced class-contact input, there is a commensurate increase in the time required to plan a course, to design and produce the support material and to provide guidance and feedback, if the same efficiency in learning is to be achieved. The main benefits are to be found in the improved convenience it offers to a particular segment of the market. Students may, of course, trade off some ease of learning for improved convenience. Correspondence courses have a long history of attracting a small but significant share of the education market, even though they are generally accepted as being a more difficult way of learning. Modern open learning techniques attempt to combine occasional contact between student and teacher with well-designed programmed learning in order to achieve an optimum mix of learning and convenience. In some circumstances a well-designed programmed learning package – computer-based or otherwise – will prove more efficient than conventional face-to-face contact in allowing students to learn at a pace which suits them best.

Pricing the product

Pricing in FHE – Constraints and Opportunities

It is commonly assumed in colleges that the fees charged for courses 'come down from on high'. It is therefore easy to neglect pricing policy in the marketing of many FHE courses. Admittedly, the local or national setting of fee levels, students grants and the like reduces the pricing autonomy of an individual college and, therefore, the level of price competition. In these circumstances, it is easy to forget that someone, somewhere is still paying for the course – even though the 'someone' may be the ratepayer rather than an individual student – and will consider its cost as a price to be paid in return for which commensurate benefits will be expected. In recent years there has also been a growth of 'full cost' courses in FHE, especially in the area of short courses for adults, in which effective pricing decisions are most definitely required. This growth looks likely to continue. The Government Consultative Paper *Commercial Activities in FE Establishments* looks forward to early legislation to remove some of the restrictions on maintained sector colleges playing a more entrepreneurial role in research and consultancy undertakings. This is likely to present more opportunities for revenue-earning college activities but also to withdraw some of the existing financial 'safety nets' in the event of failure. Given these developments, effective pricing is likely to become a major area of concern.

It is therefore becoming increasingly important that LEAs establish clear criteria within which colleges can operate in the field of pricing. An effective marketing strategy requires a prompt response to enquiries about price, and a flexibility to adjust quickly to changing circumstances in the market place.

Views may differ on the extent to which an LEA should allow a college to retain surplus revenue from full cost courses. Certainly there are powerful economic arguments in favour of ploughing investment back into successful ventures, rather than using it to prop up courses which are palpably failing to appeal to the markets for whom they are intended. Whatever the stance taken, it is clearly in everyone's interest that the degree of discretion in pricing decision making is made clear to all who are involved.

The Customer's View of Price

Seen from the viewpoint of the customers of FHE, there are a number of elements in the price of a course, each of which differs in significance to the different purchasers of the product:

— the actual fees charged to an individual student or an employer;
— student grants, allowances and other costs, paid for by the taxpayer and ratepayer, but administered by the LEA or MSC;
— the lost productivity to an employer of releasing staff to attend a course;
— the 'opportunity cost' to the student in terms of the time sacrificed to attend the course, and the resultant lost opportunities for undertaking alternative activities;
— travel, refreshment, books and other expenses incurred by the student as a result of attending a course, which may sometimes be paid for by the LEA, or by employers, as separately identified allowances;
— entry qualifications, which are a non-financial method of pricing some students out of the market-place.

For a course to be successful, the various customers and clients involved must be satisfied that the benefits gained adequately offset the price to be paid in the form of a combination of the items listed above.

Customer-derived Pricing Policy

As with the other elements of the marketing mix, an effective pricing policy starts with the customer. At present the primary means of price determination is cost-derived accounting. If the concepts of marketing are genuinely to be extended to FHE, this will need to be replaced by a pricing policy which is determined by reference to the market, the needs of the customers, their ability and willingness to pay, the availability of competitive products and the anticipated sales volume. Effective pricing is not a synonym for low prices: for some customers price will be an indicator of quality. (For instance, some FE colleges lose out to private sector competitors in the field of short management courses on the grounds of product quality and a 'down market' college image, rather than because their prices are too high).

Pricing decisions need to be taken in the light of the answers to certain questions, as indicated in Illustration 9.

Costs cannot be ignored when pricing decisions are made, even though starting from this direction is the marketing equivalent of putting the cart before the horse. In the long-run all costs need to be covered by revenue or subsidy — someone picks up the bill and is conscious of paying a price. As with the price of a product, the cost of its provision will contain

ILLUSTRATION 9 Pricing Policy Questions

- Who are your customers and clients? (Market segments, entry requirements).
- What is the price the customer will have to pay to obtain similar benefits from other providers? Alternatively, what benefits will other providers offer at a given price level? (Competition).
- Are there any special characteristics of the course which justify your charging a high or low price?
- How far is the price you charge an indicator of quality in its target markets?
- Will there be any price differentiation? (Customers charged a different price for the same product according to their willingness and ability to pay. Discounts may perhaps be offered as a means of filling vacant places).
- Should courses offered to local employers be priced lower than for others, on the grounds that the rates paid have already included an element of the price?
- Is the course a 'loss leader' and, if so, how much are you prepared to fall short of full cost recovery in order to gain a foothold with the market segment concerned?
- What is the minimum price you must charge in order to cover the full costs of the course given the forecasted level of enrolments?
- What size risks are involved if enrolment forecasts prove incorrect?

'hidden' elements which it is easy to overlook. 'Cost' is an elusive concept, capable of being identified, classified and analysed in many different ways. Most figures deemed to be a 'cost' are at best a good estimate and have built in assumptions which are sometimes questionable.

Costing Categories

FHE institutions will normally face a significant fixed cost element in terms of premises, etc. These must be met overall and it is usual for a proportional allocation to be made to each courses. On the other hand, it is still clearly worthwhile to take up spare capacity by mounting a course which only covers its direct operating costs. Similarly, the closure of a 'loss-making' course might worsen the financial position, at least in the short-term, as only heating, lighting and cleaning costs may be immediately escapable, whilst all revenue is foregone. Concepts of marginal cost and avoidable cost pricing are essential to the attraction of price sensitive market segments at a profit. Note, however, that their application to every course means that the full costs of the college business will not be recovered. It can also lead to products in their 'decline' phase being sheltered at the expense of new opportunities with healthier pricing potential. Bear in mind also that in the case of new courses a significant element of cost will be incurred prior to any enrolments of students. The most pertinent costing questions which need to be answered are indicated in Illustration 10.

Pricing, Costing and Corporate Objectives

Like the other aspects of the marketing mix, pricing should serve educational objectives rather than dictate them. Effective pricing does not necessarily imply a profit maximising policy. It will usually be quite legitimate for a college to seek to serve major market segments where the customers could never afford a 'full cost' price. Indeed, pricing below full cost is a major tool which LEAs and colleges can employ to fulfil objectives concerned with opening up access to education amongst the economically less privileged sectors of the market. Operational efficiency will still be an important consideration, however, and colleges

ILLUSTRATION 10 Costing Policy Questions

- What grades of staff will be teaching on the course? (Cost per teaching hour).
- What percentage should be added for National Insurance and Superannuation?
- What overheads do you take into account and what value is placed on them?
- Can the use of premises, non-teaching staff time and consumable materials and equipment be costed separately?
- Should overheads be allocated to courses pro rata or differentially? (To take account, for instance, of the less than proportionate use of sports facilities by part-time students).
- What have been the development costs of the course in relation to its potential lifespan?
- What are the promotional costs?
- Can these costs be specifically identified to the course in question, or are they spread over a number of courses?
- Do you have fixed ratios regarding recovery of costs or can you set your own?
- In which areas of activity are the bulk of your costs concentrated?

are being asked increasingly to account for their 'productivity' via the use of such indicators as student/staff ratios. Underpricing a course (i.e. pricing it below the level that customers are prepared to pay) may in practice only be to the short-term benefit of the customer, as additional revenue is foregone that could have been used to maintain and improve product quality. Cross-subsidisation of courses must be watched closely from this point of view. There are strong economic arguments against using surpluses from healthy and expanding courses to shore up those in terminal decline, except as a transitional arrangement prior to their 'relaunch' or replacement. Benefits to the public are likely to be higher overall if resources are invested to maintain and improve the quality of products which are established or potential successes.

Marketing and college organisation

Drawbacks of Product-Centred Organisation

Given the already noted tendency of education to be product rather than customer-centred, it is not surprising that college organisation has been determined more by the administrative requirements of those who work there than the needs of the community which it is meant to serve. Is it not significant that the word 'marketing' is virtually unknown within FHE job titles, except in the case of those staff who teach the subject?

We have already considered how the professional competence and attitudes of teaching and administrative staff can crucially affect a college's marketing capability. Clearly, the organisational and management structures in a college will also be highly relevant to the marketing effectiveness of teaching and administration, and to the ability of the institution to adapt to changing market needs.

'This means, in particular, an integrated organisation to control all customer-impinging activities. To see how far we are from such integration, consider a fairly market-conscious large college or polytechnic. Admission will be managed by staff in a central office, responsible to the registrar, in collaboration with departmental staff responsible to heads of department. Schools and industrial liaison, if they are formally recognised as separate activities in special units, are likely to be overseen by an assistant director for student services. Advertising and public relations will be handled by a small office, or perhaps just

one person, probably responsible directly to the principal or director".
(Cuthbert, R. E. *The Marketing Function in Education Management*. Coombe Lodge Working Paper IBN 1395. 1979.)

The substantial changes which have affected the market place for FHE since the mid-1970's have begun to have a noticeable impact on college organisation. To note just one example, it has become apparent that traditional structures and job specifications are often inadequate to deal with the demands placed upon them by YTS. There is also a growing acceptance in central and local government that there are financial advantages to be gained from a more considered development of the marketing function in FHE. The Audit Commission Handbook (November 1983) notes that businesses with the annual turnover of the average size FE college would expect to allocate one or two senior members of staff full-time to the marketing function.

What Kind of Organisation?

Self-inflicted organisational upheaval is an unattractive prospect to a college in the present economic climate. For some, the path forward will be based on the belief that traditional departmental organisation is incompatible with a marketing perspective. But for others radical structural changes may not be required in order to make a college more customer-orientated. Attitudinal change is more likely to be a key factor. After all, the job descriptions of some vice-principal posts contain at least an implicit recognition of the marketing function. Some heads of department could be said legitimately to have significant affinities with the 'product group manager' posts which are commonplace in business. Like product group managers, heads of department are responsible (in theory, if not always in practice) for the marketing of sub-sets of their organisations' ranges of products. The main difference between the two posts is that heads of department also fulfil the role of production managers, in that they are responsible for the day-to-day operation of the services which they market.

Some alternative structures are shown in Illustrations 11 and 12.

ILLUSTRATION 11 Marketing in a Traditional Structure

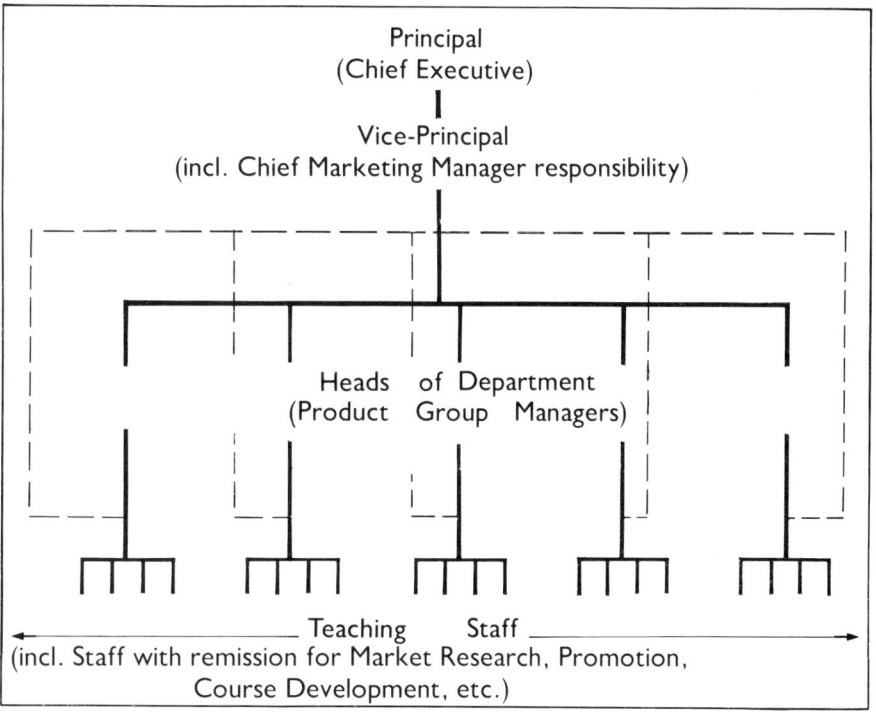

Principal
(Chief Executive)

Vice-Principal
(incl. Chief Marketing Manager responsibility)

Heads of Department
(Product Group Managers)

Teaching Staff
(incl. Staff with remission for Market Research, Promotion, Course Development, etc.)

Illustration II indicates the incorporation of marketing responsibilities within a familiar college organisational structure. The vice-principal's post is seen to incorporate the functions of a chief marketing manager, and heads of department are regarded as managers of groups of products. Certain teaching staff are given remission time in order to undertake specific marketing tasks connected with research, course development and promotion. In these areas they report directly to the vice-principal in order to ensure that corporate, rather than departmental, objectives are paramount. Otherwise, the major changes required are attitudinal — heads of department need to view their role less in terms of undying loyalty to narrowly defined subject areas and more as managers of a portfolio of courses, which will change regularly as newly developed offerings replace those which are no longer needed.

ILLUSTRATION 12 Marketing and Structural Change

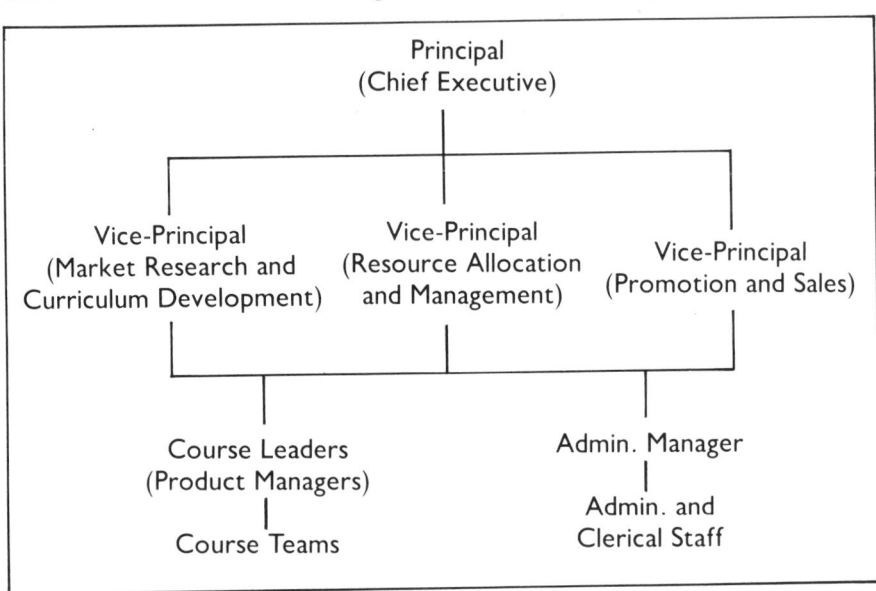

Illustration 12 provides a more committed approach, with marketing responsibilities reflected more explicitly in the organisational structure. Immediately beneath the principal, the second-tier of management is established on a functional basis. Subject-based heads of department are dispensed with and course leaders (or product managers) report directly to second-tier management, as does an administrative manager, who is responsible for the college's non-teaching staff. This structure has the advantage of giving a higher status to marketing activities overall but has the drawback of potential confusion in the 'matrix' arrangement of lines of authority between second and third-tier management.

In practice, of course, structures cannot be as rigid as is implied by any organisation chart. There must be regular liaison between departmental staff and any 'marketing specialists' over industrial liaison, admissions, new product development and so on. Similarly, a visit to an employer cannot be categorised rigidly as 'sales', as other promotion and public relations opportunities are also likely to occur. A balance has to be struck, therefore, between the creation of specialist marketing posts, and their co-ordination with the course operation side of college activity. The latter demands a management structure which encourages the development of effective course terms. Administrative boundaries which impede this development are a threat to the quality of the college's products as it is perceived by their customers.

Summary   Effective organisations are those which provide their customers with the
right products at the right place and time and at the right price. From the
customer's point of view, the 'product' is the total package which
provides the benefits which are being sought, and includes efficient
administration, job placement services and so on as well as the actual
taught course. The more those benefits can be delivered to the
customer without restrictions on location and timing, the larger is the
potential market. Customers will consider product benefits against the
perceived price they must pay. College pricing decisions are severely
constrained, but more freedom may come in the near future. A marketing perspective suggests that pricing decisions should be customer led,
but costs provide important indicators of efficiency, if treated sensibly,
and must eventually be covered by revenue or subsidy. Marketing
effectiveness can be enhanced if LEAs lay down clear guidelines to
colleges which allow for pricing flexibility in response to market trends.
Market forces are having a recognisable impact: FHE college curricula,
delivery systems and organisation are all being influenced by customer
needs. An explicit recognition of the marketing function in college
organisation would be a further step in establishing the proper
sovereignty of the customer.

4. Marketing Processes – Promoting Further Education

Synopsis

This section deals with the **promotion** of the services of FHE to their potential customers.

It starts by emphasising that effective promotion is an essential element in ensuring that the services provided by a college are taken up by the full range of people who can benefit from them. The relationship of promotion to the other elements of the **marketing mix** is then examined. The basic aim of effective promotion is summed up as **AIDA** – the creation of **attraction, interest, desire and action** amongst potential customers. It is stressed that the **techniques** outlined in the section can be **employed viably by individual colleges,** but that greater **corporate promotion** of the FHE service could provide a firmer foundation for such activities.

The techniques of **writing to persuade** are outlined in detail, using the example of a course leaflet. Stress is placed on the importance of highlighting the **benefits to the customers** and setting out information in a manner which is logical and attractive to them. **College prospectuses** and **posters** are considered on the same basis.

Paid-for **advertising** is then examined. The various **media** are described, together with **techniques for making appropriate choices.** The importance of **layout and design** to the impact of advertisements is stressed, and some basic guidance is given on achieving a clear message. **Corporate image** advertising is discussed, and the need to **monitor advertising effectiveness** is emphasised as a contribution to the effectiveness of future advertising decisions.

A short description follows of the advantages, drawbacks and techniques of **direct mail** as a form of promotion.

Personal promotion is then considered in terms of its established effectiveness, but relatively high cost. **Viable methods** are outlined which colleges can employ in the UK and overseas, as are the implications for college sales staff and their support.

Promotional events are examined next, in the form of **exhibitions, open days, conferences and organised visits.** The **cost-effectiveness** of these forms of promotion is considered, and guidance is given on **exhibition stand design, staffing, managing sales interviews,** and **undertaking subsequent debriefing and evaluation.**

Media relations are then discussed in terms of news and editorial coverage, as distinct from paid-for advertising. The importance of an **effective strategy and organisation** for media relations is examined. Guidance is given on **writing press releases** and undertaking **radio and TV**

interviews. The emphasis throughout is on the establishment of cordial and effective relationships with the media.

The section concludes with an outline of other public relations and promotion activities, including **fund raising** (both for the college and for charitable purposes), **joint promotions and sponsorships,** the maintenance of **effective student relations** and the importance of a professional approach to the **reception and entertainment of visitors.**

The place of promotion in marketing

'Too many of us have been 'taken' by the tout or con man; and all of us have been prodded into buying all sorts of 'things' we did not really need, and which we found later on we did not really want.'
(Farmer, R. N. *Would you want your daughter to marry a marketing man?* Journal of Marketing. January 1967.)

It is the area of promotion that, to many of us in education, presents the unacceptable face of marketing – the insincere approach of the 'hard-sell'. Rejection of 'marketing' is an all too easy way of assuring ourselves of our impeccable moral probity.

Yet it is in a college's publicity that education's inward-looking tendencies can be most revealed. The 'product-centred' approach is often paramount, with its implicit assumptions of the community's intrinsic interest in the courses provided. The provision of comprehensive course information, with prominently displayed 'exclusion clauses' may well be motivated by highly developed ethical considerations. But all too often it serves merely to repel attention and to quell interest before those it is aimed at have even attempted to absorb the message. This is clearly self-defeating.

The purpose of this section is to stress that effective promotion is essential if the services provided by a college are to be used by the full range of people who can benefit from them. No deception or overblown promises need be involved: simply a commitment to understanding the viewpoint of the potential customers and presenting the information in the manner which they can appreciate best. The pages which follow contain some straightforward principles and techniques which should assist colleges and LEAs to promote their services to the mutual benefit of the college, the authority and the community which they serve.

Promotion and the Marketing Mix

Promotion cannot be divorced from the other elements of the marketing mix. The **needs** of customers must have been identified clearly, and a range of products provided which will meet those needs at an appropriate price. The product must be effectively distributed or delivered to the customer. **Promotion is then the process which persuades potential customers actually to want the products or services and to take action to acquire them.** Promotion alone will not compensate for a product which does not meet customer needs, is sold at the wrong price, and is available at the wrong time and place. In these circumstances it will be at best an expensive means of propping up a declining product. Effective promotion is highly dependent on an accurate identification of the potential customers in terms of the special characteristics of the segments of the market to which a college's products will have most appeal. The better this can be done, the easier it will be in practice to select the right tool of communication with the public at the lowest cost. The various benefits offered by a college's range of services can also be segmented in order to identify the right medium and message for each part of the market.

It is also important to remember that the 'customers' of a college are buying an **intangible** product. A college 'sells' courses, certificates and diplomas – all tangible items which, if they cannot be touched or otherwise tried, can be experienced. Yet these are a means to an end for the customer, who is seeking something else, something more intangible. Students may be seeking marketable skills, career advancement and status; employers, competence, and commitment. **It is the potential benefits they will gain which persuade students and employers to make use of a course – not the course itself.**

> 'The less tangible the product, the more powerfully and persistently the judgement about it gets shaped by the packaging.'
> (Curtis, J. H. R. *Marketing Further Education*. Coombe Lodge Working Paper. IBN 1939. 1984).

A useful aide-memoire for those who have to design promotional material is AIDA – attraction, interest, desire and action.

ILLUSTRATION 13 AIDA

An effective promotion programme will need to take potential customers through four key phases. The programme must . . .

attract the	**A**ttention	of potential clients
arouse	**I**nterest	in the product
create a	**D**esire	for its benefits
prompt	**A**ction	from them in the form of a request for more information or an actual 'purchase'.

The sections which follow describe some of the promotional techniques which can be employed cost-effectively in FHE. Effective promotion strategies are quite possible even with the very limited budgets for these activities which apply in most colleges. There is little doubt, however, that a greater amount of corporate promotion of the services of FHE could do much to provide a firmer foundation for the efforts of individual colleges. Given the diversified control of the FHE service, it is hardly surprising that the public receives no strong and coherent message about the benefits which it can offer. There are also likely to be economies of scale if central bodies, LEAs and colleges co-operated in some form of corporate promotion campaign. On a more limited scale, consortia of colleges could be formed towards similar ends.

Writing to persuade
Course Leaflets

An effective way of designing a typical course leaflet is to proceed through the following stages:

— **The college is selling benefits, not a course.** It is necessary to see things through the eyes of the potential customer, their needs, their order of importance, their terms and their timing. It is important to be enthusiastic — if you aren't, it can hardly be expected of the customer.

— **The market at which the leaflet will be aimed has to be decided.** Potential students? (These can be categorised by age range — ability range — full-time/part-time/distance learning modes of study, sex). Their parents? Careers advisers? Employers? A combination of these? The more clearly the market can be defined the easier it is to design a message which it will find attractive. The more the same leaflet is aimed at different groups with distinctly different motivations, the more likely it is that all will receive a muted or confused message.

— **It is necessary to attract attention.** The leaflet cover will determine whether or not the as yet uncommitted will take a copy and read on. It need not be gimmicky to do this, but it should promise a benefit rather than assume knowledge of, and interest in, the course or the college. A course title, the name of a qualification and even the name of the college may mean nothing to many potential students.

ILLUSTRATION 14 The Leaflet Cover

BTEC HNC/D COURSES C.23 CENTRAL COLLEGE	QUALIFY FOR CAREER OPPORTUNITIES IN BUSINESS AND COMPUTING AT CENTRAL COLLEGE	GETTING LEFT BEHIND IN THE INFORMATION TECHNOLOGY RACE? CENTRAL COLLEGE CAN HELP YOU
Product centred approach — Course title, number and college name may mean nothing.	Customer-centred approach — attention attracted by the promise of career advancement.	A negative approach can be successful — the implied disadvantages of not enrolling.

A good 'house-style', including a college logo, can help re-inforce the message of the range of benefits offered by a college. It should be noted that a prominently displayed college name and logo will only attract attention where there is an established track record of delivery of certain benefits — in the same way that the British Rail double-arrow symbol has become an effective cypher for certain established benefits of rail travel. However, for most potential students and most colleges, the college name and logo of themselves will not convey the promise of any benefits. The idea of education is not immediately attractive to most people, and may be actively repellent to some.

— **Interest must be aroused and desire created** by describing simply and clearly how the course will supply the promised benefits. Once again, it is important not to assume knowledge where it may not exist — this means that initials which are very familiar in FHE (BTEC, CGLI, HND, YTS, etc.) need to be explained. The minimum information necessary to be persuasive should be given in as straightforward a way as possible to those the course is intended to serve. Lengthy and complex explanations tend to kill interest at the outset and, if they are necessary, can always be dealt with at a later stage when an initial commitment has been secured and an enquiry made. Wherever possible, the potential customer should be addressed as an individual, using a positive and personal approach. A logical ordering from the viewpoint of the potential student is indicated in Illustration 15.

ILLUSTRATION 15 The Leaflet's Contents

- Enlarge on the benefits promised on the cover of the leaflet, in terms of career enhancement and other benefits.
- Describe what the student will learn, setting out the course content in layman's terms. Module and unit titles which may only be meaningful to the teacher should be avoided.
- State how the student will learn by describing ways of studying, times of attendance, workload involved, the degree of choice and other features.
- Indicate *what* the student will *get out of it* by explaining the qualification(s) which can be gained, and the exemptions, equivalances and opportunities for progression which the studies offer. (Formal certification may be non-existent or unimportant in the case of some courses, and here the stress can be placed instead on the usefulness of the knowledge and skills acquired).
- Explain why the student should study at this college. Establish the college's credentials, provide evidence of the quality of teaching staff and resources, plus details of ancillary features such as the student union and sports facilities. Quotes from previous 'satisfied customers' can usefully be included here.
- Explain what the student needs to enter the course, giving details of any entry requirements and fees. The opportunity should be taken to refer students who are under- or over-qualified for entry to suitable alternative courses also offered by the college.
- Finally, it is useful to close by restating the most important benefit of the course to the customer.

— **Action should be prompted by giving details of how, where and when to enrol, and how to obtain further information.** There should be a friendly invitation to enquire further, and the college should be capable of dealing efficiently with those who are persuaded by the leaflet to find out more. The leaflet has not succeeded if it does not lead to any further action on the part of those at which it is aimed. It will equally have failed if subsequent enquiries are met with remarks such as 'He's teaching at the moment — I don't know anything

about that course. Can you ring back later?' Faced with this type of response, many enquirers will not pursue matters any further. Contacts quoted in leaflets should normally be available to deal with queries, and there should be known alternates to whom reference can be made when they are not.

– **Good design will be assisted by a simple, attractive layout.** It is necessary to consider what needs to be said in terms of the number of pages/folds in the leaflet. It may be possible to cut down copy in order to reduce cost. 'White space' is useful to break up columns of print, but too much is wasteful – it is wise to make sure that it is filled to best advantage. Photographs and colour can enhance attractiveness, but will also increase costs.

– **Testing the 'rough' of a course leaflet** on a sample of potential customers can be advantageous in identifying confusions and omissions in the copy and in judging its basic appeal to its target market. This can allow effective refinements to be made before going to print.

– **Planning ahead is vital if the timing of publication is to be right for the target population.** It is necessary to work backwards from printers' timescales and allow some 'recovery' margin for delays. Techniques such as critical path analysis can contribute to the planning of publication timing.

The College Prospectus

The college prospectus is potentially a crucial promotional document for the institution. Bristol Polytechnic, with an average of twenty applicants for every available place, regards its prospectus as a particularly important source of information for school-leavers. It can be thought of as a multiple leaflet, to which the techniques outlined above are equally applicable. It is doubtful if many colleges view it in these terms, given the excessive emphasis placed in most prospectuses on 'what the college is doing' rather than on 'what the college can do for you'. The layout of information in a prospectus all too often reflects college departmental priorities and boundaries, rather than the characteristics of different market segments, and unexplained initials and jargon proliferate. From the viewpoint of the potential student, it is helpful to have information presented in convenient groupings – by age/ability range, career, full/part-time, and so on – and to provide plenty of cross-references. Short summaries should be provided in each section so that detailed information can be avoided until interest has been clearly established.

It can be claimed that market segmentation would be made more effective by replacing the traditional prospectus with shorter and more specific brochures. The College for the Distributive Trades, for instance, has separate full-time and part-time course prospectuses, since it was found that these markets were in practice quite distinct from each other. However, for some colleges there may be good reasons for retaining the traditional approach.

'We have had many discussions over the format of the college prospectus, but the argument which always wins the day is that we should retain a traditional composite prospectus on the grounds that (1) training officers in larger industries prefer all the information in one single source rather than spread over a number of booklets or leaflets and (2) a prospectus taken by an enquirer is then passed round the family and friends who may see an activity in which they are interested, rather than that single interest of the original enquirer.' (Bill Easton, Principal, Southgate Technical College).

Posters The techniques of persuasive copy writing also need to be applied in the design of posters. Indeed, as there is relatively less space to put over the college's message, it becomes even more important to focus on the key points of interest to the potential customer. Handbill type posters, for display on notice-boards, can sensibly contain more copy than hoardings, where only a very basic message can be conveyed to passers-by. Nonetheless, the latter type of poster can be very effective in promoting a positive image of a particular product, service or concept. An immediate visual appeal is very important if posters are to have any real effect. This can be enhanced by using copy sparingly in a bold and memorable style.

Advertising

Media Newspapers, magazines, journals and posters provide colleges with their main vehicles of paid-for advertising. It is unlikely that TV[6] will ever be an affordable avenue for most colleges, but local radio and cinema might well prove cost-effective for certain markets. Other advertising possibilities include panels on buses, taxis and parking-meters, slogans on tee-shirts, envelope franking and even the backs of bus tickets. The cost of buying space and time makes it even more important than in the case of a leaflet that the message is kept short and simple, with the most attractive benefits well to the fore. The same basic AIDA principles

apply. The advantage of these methods of promotion lies overwhelmingly in the mass markets which can be reached – a 1% response rate to an advertisement appearing in a newspaper which is read by 25,000 people still represents a significant number of enquiries in terms of a single college. The unit cost per reader in printed media is usually extremely low, but the minimum advertising investment needed to ensure impact in the target market sectors can be high in the context of the modest publicity budget of most colleges.

An essential source of reference in making decisions on buying space and time is the regularly updated **British Rate and Data (BRAD)** which contains full details of the cost of advertising in the UK mass media, together with audited circulation figures. The Blue Book of British Broadcasting, which lists every programme on every radio and TV station in the UK, is also useful. It is especially important that the target market for an advertisement is identified if value for money is to be obtained from the choice of media. Sixteen-year-old school-leavers may well not read the local paper: their parents may, however, and they may be influential in the decision to enrol.

Similarly, the relatively small numbers of employers who take the decisions which effectively determine the enrolment for some part-time vocational courses may be reached best via restricted circulation trade journals. It is necessary to answer three questions when making advertising decisions:
– which people most influence the decision to enrol on this course?
– what do they read or listen to?
– when are they most likely to be interested in the course?

The first two questions are concerned with targeting the advertisement on the right sector of the market, the third is concerned with **timing**: it is clearly best to advertise at the times when 'buying' decisions are most likely to be taken.

Layout and Design

The layout and design of an advertisement should be considered in relation to realistic goals. In newspapers and leisure interest magazines, a college's advertisement will be competing for the readers' attention with many others – it must be attention-grabbing if it is not to be passed over. Most readers will not be predisposed to hear about education. A limited, straightforward and simple message is needed, calculated to arouse maximum interest in the target population. This applies even more to broadcasting – very few separate pieces of information can be absorbed by listeners in the space of, say, a thirty second radio advertisement. The more facts are crammed in, the more risk there is that nothing registers. In the case of careers and training journals, more detail can be included in an advertisement without killing interest, since readers have already indicated a disposition to want information in this area. The message may need re-inforcement if action is to be prompted. Experience will help to determine the optimum number of insertions of the same advertisement. Copy and graphics for advertisements should be in scale to the space being purchased to assist the typesetter to keep to the design which you intended.

A further possibility when considering newspapers is the advertising feature, whereby space for articles concerning the college is paid for by associated advertising. Advertising features can be a useful occasional alternative to straightforward press advertising, but they are not as valuable as genuine editorial copy, which is dealt with in the section 'Using the Media'.

Corporate Image Advertising

Most college advertising tends to be directed towards prompting enquiries and enrolments for a particular course or courses. Corporate image advertising is also a potentially advantageous method of promotion, although its effects are likely to be more long-term and difficult to monitor accurately. Here the college as a whole puts forward a message of having something to offer everyone in the community. Employers may be offered the general promise of solutions to training problems, rather than being directed to specific courses. By continual reinforcement, the image of a thriving and successful college becomes established in the public mind, and is recalled when a need for education arises. This will not happen, of course, if there is no substance beneath the image which is projected; but a college which has the right 'products' and is genuinely responsive to new needs can ensure that success breeds success by keeping its (good) name in the public eye in this way. In the same way, it is possible to promote the benefits of education in general, and that offered by the FHE service in particular, all of which has a potential spin-off for the local college.

Monitoring Advertising Effectiveness

The unit cost of obtaining responses to an advertisement in terms of further enquiries and enrolments is a crucial indicator of the relative efficiency of the competing channels of communication. This can be monitored by asking those who follow up the advertisement to mention where they saw it. An alternative way of achieving the same end is to incorporate a reply slip in the advertisement which, when sent to the college, will allow its source to be identified. It should be remembered that it is the number of additional enrolments eventually achieved which justifies the advertisement — and one enquiry from an employer may lead to multiple and continued part-time enrolments.

Direct mail

Leaflets will not promote if they are not seen by the potential customers. If they are confined to college premises, and to conferences, exhibitions and open days, they will preach to those who are already at least partially committed. Circulation via public libraries, schools, youth centres and the careers service is a means of widening the contact with prospective students. Direct mail shots can be used to seek individual students, and to attract support from employers, but costs need to be considered carefully against the likely response rate.

If direct mailing of promotional literature is to take place regularly, an efficiently maintained mailing list is essential. Some commercially produced mailing lists are expensive and of dubious accuracy. A college is likely to find greater benefits if its own mailing list is developed from such sources as its known contacts with employers, the chamber of commerce, trade associations, community groups and from regional industrial directories. Alternatively, it may be possible to take advantage of a mail shot carried out by one of these organisations to distribute college literature at little or no cost. Another alternative might be to offset costs by selling space in the mailshot to commercial or other groups. Ideally, promotional literature should be addressed to a named individual within each organisation. This means that mailing lists need to be updated regularly.

The full cost of direct mail publicity is often overlooked. In some colleges, the cost of postage is allocated to the general administrative budget rather than the publicity budget. The stamp, however, is often a more expensive item than the leaflet which is being mailed. The main advantage of direct mail is its selectivity — it allows publicity material to

be targeted directly. Provided mailing lists are accurate, and the material used is attention grabbing, it can be very cost-effective. Otherwise, material may never reach its intended readership or be consigned immediately to the water paper bin.

Personal promotion

Advantages and Disadvantages

Personal contact (face-to-face or by telephone) is usually the most effective promotion technique in terms of the number of actual responses as a proportion of the number of contacts. Because it is possible to engage in a dialogue with the potential customer, the message can be tailored to arouse maximum interest and desire in the individual concerned. Initial attention is easier to attract — appointments can be arranged, and natural politeness will prevent most people from totally refusing to listen. The presence of the 'salesman' can help overcome the inertia that prevents interest being converted into action in non-personal forms of promotion. There is, however, one major drawback — it is by far the most costly method judged by the time needed to make contact with each customer (as high as £50 per man-hour at current prices, depending on the staff involved). Even assuming a much lower rate, the cost of one employer interview can quite easily be around £200 once time is added for travelling, planning, debriefing and associated administration. If half such interviews are successful in terms of maintaining or creating custom (and this represents a very healthy 'conversion rate' judged by commercial standards) then the average contribution per contact must be £400 in order to break even. Personal selling time must therefore be used productively in combination with non-personal forms of communication.

Effective Methods of Personal Promotion

For colleges, personal contact will be most effective in the following cases.

- Where one contact can lead to many customers. This can apply to individual employers, training advisers, careers officers, MSC officers, and the like. Contact with LEA officers can also be seen in this light, since the LEA is the major funder of the college on behalf of the local community. It is worth allocating time to contacts which help to ensure adequate resourcing as this in turn will help to attract students. Schools are also potential suppliers of significant numbers of students: the development of amicable relationships with neighbouring secondary schools, working to an agreed local strategy, with the college represented at their careers guidance sessions, can prove a highly cost-effective method of personal promotion.

- Where it is possible for one person to contact many potential customers in a short space of time. This can apply to careers conferences, exhibitions and open days.

ILLUSTRATION 16 Do's and Don'ts of Personal Promotion

- Don't mistake pleasant conversation for effective promotion.
- Don't waste large amounts of expensive staff time on contacts with restricted potential.
- Don't spend time trying to create interest in a course which clearly will not fit the needs of the contact.
- Don't continue a dialogue unnecessarily once the desired result has been obtained. Continued attention to customers has an important role in promotion, but it should be kept in proportion.
- Do keep to the point and concentrate on the benefits you can offer to your contact. Many useful contacts are busy people themselves and will appreciate a professional approach which is relevant without being brusque.
- Do make sure you are speaking to someone who influences enrolment decisions. In a large firm you may be directed to the Training Officer, but policy on day release may actually reside with the line managers.

Sales Staff and their Support

It is important to bear in mind that the potential customer will view a salesperson as a representative of the college. An interview may have been arranged with the aim of securing enrolments on an engineering course, but the contact may also express interest in secretarial courses. A negative and defensive response at this point is a lost sales opportunity for the college. Some establishments offer successful help to staff involved in personal contacts by means of a college 'sales manual' which provides guidance on the message to be conveyed and how to put it across, together with all the information which the potential customer might require. An example of this approach is given in Illustration 17. Another method is to make one or more members of staff specifically responsible for external liaison, allowing them to develop knowledge of the full range of college services, and expertise in promoting them in the right quarters.

ILLUSTRATION 17 Support to Sales Staff — Longlands College Industrial Liaison Pack

The industrial liaison pack which has been developed at Longlands College in Middlesbrough is aimed at enabling selected staff to present the college to industry in a professional and consistent manner. It consists of the following features:

- a series of aides-memoire to help the representative to give a polished presentation of the college's facilities;
- a series of up-to-date print-outs showing the full range of current college capability in all departments;
- short course programmes from across the department with which the representative is particularly involved;
- photographs and display materials showing the college, its work and its facilities;
- a give-away folder summarising the work of the college and presented to the industrial contact at the first visit.

The pack is used in conjunction with an industrial database which the college has established using a BBC(B) micro-computer.
A comprehensive record of industrial liaison is thereby retained on easy to retrieve computer records.

By using the liaison pack, the college hopes that lecturers visiting industry will:

- be able to make a more professional presentation to potential clients;
- be able to represent the college as a whole rather than narrow specialist interests;
- demonstrate the total range of facilities available in the college which may not be appreciated by prospective clients;
- leave a permanent reminder of the college, its capability, its professionalism and its range of activities.

The college also hopes to develop a presentation video or slide package to be used in conjunction with the liaison pack.

Personal Promotion In Overseas Markets

The main means for recruiting overseas students have traditionally been personal contacts, both directly through past students and through institutional contacts with influential decision-makers in overseas countries; and indirectly, through UK-based organisations with international links and roles, such as the British Council. Occasional forays have been undertaken by individuals promoting a particular course or department in a UK institution. These may have involved little more than a speculative visit to those local academic institutions which might provide potential students. A rather more organised approach has been to advertise the recruiter's presence at a local hotel through newspapers and elsewhere, and then to interview potential students. A variant of this has been to use a local agent to make contact with potential students. Such casual approaches have attracted criticisms when open competition between rival institutions has led to mutual disparagement. This is a further argument, in addition to cost saving, for collaborative initiatives overseas.

Promotional events – Exhibitions, open days and conferences

Types of Event

Exhibitions, open days and (in some cases) conferences represent unique promotional events at which advertising and personal selling can be focused on a large number of potential customers in a relatively short space of time. More immediate impact can be achieved than with conventional mail shots and media advertisements. If the venue is the right one, it can be the most cost-effective form of promotion

There are three basic types of promotional event:

– **General** (e.g. a Local Authority mounted exhibition of community services): general events usually involve a larger number of visitors, but many of them may not be potential customers. Hence it is necessary to ascertain the potential of the event before committing significant time and money to an exhibition of this nature.

– **Trade** (e.g. a Careers Convention): here a large percentage of visitors are potential customers – the nature of the event will inevitably attract those who are predisposed to interest in college products.

– **Private** (e.g. a college open day): here all the advantages of full control of the operation present themselves. The college can decide the audience to be invited and the exact time of the event. Elaborate displays can be mounted at a relatively low cost. On the other hand, it may be more difficult to attract large numbers of potential customers to a purely college-sponsored event. Continued promotion to existing customers has an important place but there is no point in preaching only to the already converted. Some colleges – such as Bristol Polytechnic – regard conducted parties of smaller groups of potential customers during normal working hours as a more effective form of promotion than a conventional open day. Visits from school parties may be dealt with more appropriately by this approach.

The types of visitor who are likely to attend any of these events need to be identified so that the benefits of the most appropriate range of courses can be promoted. It is also useful to consider the 'competition' in the form of other colleges and training establishments which might be present.

Cost-effectiveness

The costs of promotional events can be substantial, even if all that is involved is the hire of a small stand at an exhibition organised by another party. In addition to the direct costs of the exhibition space, stand hire, support materials and staffing, there are significant 'hidden' costs in the considerable amount of planning which such events require if they are to go smoothly. It is necessary to ensure value for money. Prime sites for exhibition stands are on main 'traffic flows' near catering, bar and toilet facilities, or adjacent to other major, but non-competing exhibitors.

To be effective, exhibition literature must, of course, fulfil the AIDA criteria. There should be plenty of cheap material for 'collectors', with more expensive leaflets kept for those who express interest and appear more likely to 'buy'. Leaflets should be readily available to passers-by — for instance, by means of a dispenser. If there are major sales opportunities, it may be worthwhile to incorporate a tape-slide, film or video presentation, or to demonstrate the use of a computer terminal, or some other item of college equipment.

Stand Design

The design of the exhibition stand should aim at maximum visual impact, conveying instantly the main benefits on offer and where they can be obtained. The stand should be open, light, attractive and inviting, but carpeted and well furnished to look durable and safe in the eyes of the customer. Lettering should be clear, large and at eye level, with the use of only a few succint and striking words. Speed and ease of erection will help with stands designed for flexible re-use at future events.

Staffing — a Professional Approach

Staff manning the stand should be briefed not only on their own 'products' but on their target market in general. Training in inter-personal skills will assist staff in maintaining a professional image at all times. Existing 'customers' should be capable of being identified in order to prevent confusion and duplication, and to sustain the business-like impression.

Spin-offs

Booking space at general or trade events offers significant spin-offs in terms of learning from experience and from other exhibitors. It is sensible to use 'off-stand' time to visit other stands, in order to gain market intelligence, and to note good promotional ploys.

The Visitors

Successful exhibition stands are manned by staff who understand the psychology of the visitor and can match their approach to it. It is important to remember from the start that the visitor is unlikely to feel 'at home' — the event is alien territory. Some visitors may already have definite ideas on the information they require, in which case they are unlikely even to approach your stand unless they are seeking your type of product, or are attracted by the immediate visual impact of the stand. Many will not have a very clear aim, however, and may be just passing time away. They are likely to feel shy, reluctant to be seen looking at your stand and drawing attention to themselves, reluctant to enter your 'territory', reluctant to talk (at least at first), unwilling to disturb your immaculate display of literature, and happy to accept leaflets handed to them and flee. It will only take three to six seconds for a visitor to pass your stand, so there is limited time for these barriers to be overcome.

It follows from this that the basic message must be communicated quickly. The stand design itself must do this. Leaflets and other promotional materials should be within easy reach without the visitor having to enter the stand. Staff manning the stand should be open and welcoming, whilst avoiding over-eagerness by clustering and pouncing. The entrance should not be blocked with bodies or furniture! Some hints on managing a sales interview are set out in Illustration 18.

ILLUSTRATION 18 Managing the Sales Interview

- Approach visitors: open the conversation, rather than waiting for them to approach you. Stand to address visitors, maintaining eye contact with them. Visitors can be invited to sit to discuss business.
- Identify the visitor's needs: avoid remarks like 'Can I help you?' as an opening gambit – they invite a negative response which closes the conversation. Employ open questions instead and encourage them to question you. Show interest in the visitors and their questions – show them that they are important to you. Identify yourself and your role. Identify the visitor – some will have a business card. Identify the visitor's interests and needs. Decide quickly if you are the best suited to deal with the visitor, then continue or pass them on politely to a colleague.
- Negotiate the 'sale': promote the product(s) which best meet the customer's needs, and discuss the benefits which they can offer.
- Close the sale: agree action and follow-up with the customer, in terms of actual enrolment or the supply of further information.
- Close the interview: develop polite 'closing-ploys'. While you are talking to people who don't want your courses, or who have already been persuaded, other potential customers may pass by and be lost.

Debriefing and Evaluation

It is sensible to hold a debriefing on the event while it is fresh in the minds of those who attended – ideas for future improvements can then be aired. A critical evaluation can be carried out later in the light of evidence of the amount of positive response which was produced. If the response rate has not been cost-effective, it is important to decide the key reasons for failure – the wrong event? The wrong type of visitor? Or faults in the design and operation of the stand(s)? If the event in question has proved a success, should more space be taken next time?

Using the media

Relations with the Media

Press and other media relations should form an integral part of a college's comprehensive marketing and public relations strategy. Contrary to the generally held view, coverage by the local media of colleges' activities and provision can generally be obtained reasonably easily. Newspapers and local radio are the most accessible media and through them colleges can reach a wider audience than through traditional forms of promotion.

This is not to say that press relations is an easy business. It has certain limitations and, in particular, it is much less controllable than other forms of promotion. However, armed with an appropriate strategy for press relations and some skills which are relatively easily learned, colleges should be able to maximise the advantages and minimise the disadvantages of working with the media. As a starting point it is important to bear in mind that, whilst there is little public (and that includes the press) understanding of FE, a well managed, systematic approach to the media can promote the college – and an image of further education in general – as dynamic, caring, relevant to people and responsive to local needs.

The media consists of local and national newspapers, local and national radio (both commercial and the BBC) and regional and national television. In recent years there has been an upsurge in the development of media which may be particularly relevant to colleges: free newspapers, the papers and newsletters of community groups, tenants associations, ethnic groups, women's organisations, etc., and the publications of professional bodies and special interest groups. Coverage by the media does not just involve news stories. Letters to the press, calls to radio phone-in programmes, interviews and the feature articles are all useful forms of publicity.

Different elements of the media need to be approached in different ways and an essential part of a college's promotional strategy will be knowing its local media and having some idea of the nature of the audience reached by the different elements. For example, some small scale exposure on local radio might achieve much greater effect on the 16-18 age group than a large scale feature in the local paper. Whether the audience at which you are aiming is general or specific will depend on the particular marketing objective you have at any point in time.

What makes News?

'News is people'
(Harold Evans)

It is critical to remember that, whilst events happen, news is **made** and the vast bulk of news is about people. Any media strategy needs to take that into account since it informs the approach colleges need to make to the press. The fact that a particular course is on offer at the college for the fifth year running, or even that a new course is being put on, is hardly likely to stimulate any interest. However, the fact that a graduate from the course has won a national prize or gained a particular job, or that the new course has been put on to meet the needs of a local firm or community group, might well be newsworthy. Coverage is most likely to be achieved if the 'angle' used is right. Not all news has to be local in origin, even for the local media. For example, the launching of the national Youth Training Scheme attracted much publicity in areas where a local angle could be taken. It is not difficult to see why since it had all the key newsworthy ingredients. It was a new scheme for unemployed young people, it was aimed at a particular kind of recruit and it relied on relations with other organisations and firms in the community. Essentially, it was easy to focus on the novelty and on the people involved.

Having said that news is people, it is also important to bear in mind that different elements of the media have their own news values. An important part of a media strategy is to know the different criteria which the media operate in deciding what to publish, These criteria can be gleaned through regular attention to the media and also by getting to know the editors, reporters and broadcasters concerned. One thing no newspaper will do is to act as a free college prospectus. All newspapers, and especially free ones, rely on advertising revenue and they are not in the business of providing free advertisements. It is therefore unlikely that bombarding the press with prospectuses or leaflets, unaccompanied by any news or feature story, will achieve any coverage whatsoever.

Organising to deal with the Media

A key element in a press or media relations strategy is the organisation a college establishes for dealing with and responding to the media. All colleges should have at least one press, publicity or information officer. This not only ensures a systematic and uniform approach but also gives the media an easily accessible contact inside the college. Since media relations is a two-way process this is crucial. It may be that the press officer is a member of the college's senior management team, or someone appointed specifically to do that job. In any event it is a professional job and it requires time and resources.

The press officer's job will be impossible unless he or she receives material from the different parts of the college in sufficient detail to allow its conversion into publicity which will attract coverage. The press officer, and others working with him or her (e.g. departmental liaison staff), will need training in the ways of interesting the media in the college and in dealing with journalists who are not there just to give the college a good press. Judgements have to be made on what to publicise and how. Skill in dealing with journalists is essential. An untutored approach or response to some questions posed by journalists can lead to misleading reports, a bad press or over-sensational reporting. What is told to journalists 'on the record', 'off the record' and 'not for quoting' needs to be handled sensitively, especially if the journalist in question is not known to the informant. All this underlines the need for the proper organisation of media relations, for the training of those involved, and for clearly understood and widely known college rules about who is permitted to deal with the media and on what.

Getting to know the Media

It is also underlines the need to know the media. The yellow pages should provide the contact telephone numbers of the local press, radio and television. All papers themselves contain contact 'phone numbers. Most papers will be glad to establish a professional link with the college and a 'phone call should be all that is necessary to establish that link, especially if accompanied by an invitation to the college. Alternatively, a press release could be the basis for the first contact followed by a telephone call asking about its receipt and likely coverage. The news editor will give advice on who you should meet and whether there is a specialist education reporter or one with education as part of a wider brief.

In addition to assessing local media news values, as indicated above, a study should be made of press content and style. Are the articles long or short? Does the paper have a record of interest in education, training, employment and so on? Does it regularly publish features? Does it have columns devoted, for example, to young people, ethnic minorities, women?

It is clearly important in dealing with the ethnic minority press to know the language in which the paper appears. The simple step of having a story or press release translated into that language will greatly increase its chances of being picked up.

A fundamental piece of information is the deadline. It is necessary to know when to send in a story and worth remembering that letters and features pages are usually 'put to bed' before the news pages of newspapers. Observing deadlines is crucial. Even if a story is good, coverage will be sacrificed by submitting it a day late.

The College's Media Profile

A key item of the strategy which needs to be considered is the nature of the media profile the college wishes to project. That decision, again, needs to rest on the college's overall marketing objectives. If a high profile is sought then every activity in which the college is engaged, from open days to the initiation of research or commercially linked projects, should be seen as potential media material. A new project with a local firm, the creation of a short course for a particular group of people or employers, individual examination successes, the winning of prizes, the non-college achievements of students and staff, the arrival of new staff, the achievement of new jobs by existing staff and the celebration of long service can all be reported.

The strategy to be adopted by the college needs to be discussed with the LEA. The LEA will have its own press relations arrangements, which need to be integrated with the college's organisation. Similarly, bodies like NATFHE have well-developed national and local media relationship and can offer advice and assistance with some aspects of the college's media work.

Some stories and features will touch on sensitive areas as will some enquiries from reporters. The college needs to know how and when to seek guidance from the LEA in many of these cases. For example, the problems caused by lack of resources may be very newsworthy. An approach to the LEA in advance of any comment on an item such as this can avoid a later conflict and might result in a story mutually acceptable to the college and the LEA. It is also important to be aware of LEA policies on media relations and of the use which can be made of the LEA or local authority press office.

Writing Press Releases

The most important form of communication with the media (including radio and TV) is the issuing of press releases. There are some tricks of the trade in writing a release, and an indication of the key features of a typical press release are set out in Illustration 19. It can be used as a checklist for those who have to write or draft releases. However, some particular points worth stressing are set out below:

- The release must have a good headline which attracts immediate interest. This is the only part of many releases which is actually read, prior to their consignment to the waste bin! To avoid this fate the headline must be eye-catching and sum up the item in question. It is important to remember that the headline is not written for inclusion in the paper; that is the sub-editor's job. The purpose of the headline is to catch the editor's attention.

- The release needs an angle. Make it people-centred and locally orientated, especially for the local and regional press, radio and TV.

- The first paragraph is crucial. In many cases only the first paragraph will be used so it should contain the bones of your message. In general, the bottom sections of a release are more likely to be cut than the top sections.

- The first paragraph should state **who** the information is about, **what** you are publicising, **why** (if it is an event) the event has occurred, **where** and **when** it has happened, or **will** happen, and (if it is a course) **when** it will start.

- The release should be short (rarely over one page) with wide margins and double spacing.

- The release should be succinct and contain a quote or quotes from an individual, whether it's the principal, head of department, member of staff or a student.

- A clear black and white photo with a caption will always increase the chance of publication, particularly if the caption points out 'local' people.

- Any embargo should be clearly marked at the top of the release. The end of the release should be marked by the word 'ENDS' at the bottom of the release and the day and night telephone number of a contact for further information should be given. It is necessary to make sure that this contact is available when the journalist receives the release.

ILLUSTRATION 19 A Typical Press Release

to show when story can be published

origin of the release

FOR IMMEDIATE RELEASE

BILDEANE COLLEGE OF FURTHER EDUCATION
121 Hazelton Road, Bildeane, Blotshire

first para' contains the five w's

New College Course Brings Job Finding Success

who *why* *where* *what* *when*

70% of women who attended a new style course at Bildeane College have either found jobs or secured places in further education, according to a survey released today (2nd February) by the College.

The course - the first of its kind at the College - was designed to help women considering going back to work or returning to education after being at home for some time.

The course included information and advice on job opportunities, job sampling, vists to employers, Maths and English brush up sessions and career counselling. A creche was available throughout the course.

Of the 20 women attending, 14 (70%) had found jobs, 6 of them were also attending further education classes on day release or in the evenings, 2 had taken temporary jobs prior to starting full-time further education courses. 7 of the 14 had part-time jobs and 7 were working full-time. 4 women had been unable to find a job and 2 had been prevented from looking for work because of domestic crises.

MORE

to show there is another page

name in full

Mary Harris, a former student on the course said:

'I saw a leaflet about the course in the launderette. I haven't had any education since I left school 15 years ago so I was really nervous about applying. I'm really glad I did. I've now got a clerical job with Bildeane Jeans and I'm taking classes in book keeping and English O-level at the college'.

quote

ENDS — To show there is no more to come

2nd February 1985 — Always date the release

For further information contact:-

Jenny Lacey,

Course Cordinator

Bildeane (0986) 2191 - college

0532 6872 - home

Contact name and telephone numbers

useful supplementary information

Note to Editors

The course attended by the women was a 'Wider Opportunities for Women' course under the Manpower Services Commission, Training Opportunities Scheme. It ran for 6 weeks during October and November 1984 on a full-time basis.

Radio and TV Interviews   Much of what has been said above, (particularly about releases), applies to radio and television. If radio or TV interest can be gained it will probably be necessary to provide someone who can be interviewed. It is as well to prepare for this in advance. Further, just as letters to the press are a useful and under-used publicity device so, too, are phone-in slots on local and national radio.

Radio and TV interviewing makes people nervous but, armed with a few ground rules, some training and preparation, the exercise is not so intimidating as it at first appears. Recorded interviews give the interviewee an advantage — the interviewee should feel free to have passages re-recorded if his or her point has not been made well. Equally, it gives broadcasters an advantage since they can select passages for broadcasting! So the interviewer should be asked how long the piece is likely to be when it goes out, and keep what is said as close to that as possible. They have much more freedom to edit if they are given the chance. The first sentence should be very powerful; most radio is like wallpaper and it is not heeded properly unless the listener is motivated.

The motivation comes in the first line. It should be remembered that the broadcast is received by small groups of people in their own home, so don't lecture to a full house. Radio and TV is received very personally.

If live broadcasting is to take place, it is crucial that the interviewer insists that the journalist runs through, in advance, the questions to be asked. If certain angles are to be avoided these must be made clear prior to the interview as part of the terms on which the interview is to take place. A preliminary talk before any interview is crucial and it is important to regard that talk as equivalent to the press release in relation to a newspaper story. Initials (e.g. C&G and CNAA) and technical terms should be avoided, and it is important to remember that in the short time available points will only be made comprehensively if they are presented logically, simply and (above all) briefly. Some colleges have acquired a regular 'spot' on local radio. This can be linked with careers advice or more general youth counselling by using the phone-in format. Most local radio stations have two district areas of output, News and Programmes. Two press releases, at least, should therefore be sent, preferably by name to each programme presenter who might use them.

The Media Partnership

A great deal can be gained from a well-organised strategy towards media relations. Poor organisation, or a total absence of it, does not stop coverage. It simply leads, at best, to an uncontrolled press and, more likely, to a thoroughly bad press. However, press relations is a two way process and, once established, places the college in an obligation to deal with issues it would not usually wish to pursue publicly. 'No comment' can be, and may need to be, used in respect of certain scandals, but as a ploy it needs to be carefully rationed: otherwise the partnership will fold.

Other public relations and promotion issues

There are many aspects of the contact between a college and its local community which are not directly concerned with selling courses, but which nevertheless contribute towards the establishment and main-tenance of a positive image. The acceptance of invitations to speak to Rotary Clubs, Chambers of Commerce and local community groups, and the involvement of the college in charitable fund-raising activities are just some examples.

'The college also participates in a number of charitable activities. Last year some £2,700 was raised by students and staff and distributed to

local charities. The college theatre is used for a number of external charitable functions and these attract many more visitors to the college . . . our Catering Studies Department assists a number of local organisations, particularly during December, by cooking and serving special meals. All the foregoing helps to establish the name and reputation of the college in the vicinity'.
(Bill Easton, Principal, Southgate Technical College).

Fund raising for the college itself provides more direct opportunities to remind the local community of the range of benefits which are offered. Such initiatives must be used sparingly, however, if their impact is to be optimised and if resentment resulting from constant requests for money is to be avoided. Applications for specific funding from MSC, FEU and other central bodies also need to be considered as a form of promotion. Slipshod presentation of submissions for funds casts doubt on the institution's professionalism and jeopardises their chance of success, whatever the intrinsic merits of the proposals concerned. The same principle applies to submissions where no funding is involved, as in the case with proposals to BTEC or the CNAA.

Joint promotional activities and commercial sponsorships are also being pursued by some colleges to their benefit. The addition of an educational message to a better known commercial promotion, backed by a much larger budget, can have advantages for all concerned. An example of this approach is the 'Adult Education is for Skolars' caravan used in Birmingham LEA as a result of sponsorship from Allied Breweries, the makers of Skol Lager.

Evidence indicates that word of mouth is one of the most significant avenues via which interest in a course is awakened in potential students. It is often said that a college's students are its best advertisements, and there is some truth in this statement. A positive, efficient and helpful attitude to students during their course can bear fruit in recommendations to friends to follow their example. The maintenance of contact with past students also has an important spin-off in this direction.

Finally, the first impressions which a college presents to its visitors are a vital complement to well-taught and efficiently administered courses. An uninviting reception area, organised to give an impression of indifference to all but the convenience of the college, is one of the easiest ways of acquiring a bad reputation in the eyes of potential customers within an instant of their crossing the threshold. The absence of properly appointed interview rooms, and of the capability to entertain visitors according to their status, can also reinforce this shabby and unprofessional image, especially in the eyes of industrial clients. A penny-pinching approach to expenditure in these areas may therefore prove to be an entirely false economy.

Summary

Promotion is a vital part of the marketing process. The benefits of products which meet genuine customer needs, and are available at the right price, place and time, need to be communicated effectively to the potential customer if they are to be taken up fully.

This need not be a matter of slick or glossy presentation, snappy wording or hard-sell ploys, but simply presenting possible customers with the facts they need, in an order logical to them, and in a manner which will make them want to take advantage of the facilities offered — to your mutual benefit.

Successful promotion needs to secure AIDA from the customer — attention, interest, desire and action. To achieve this it is necessary to place the emphasis on the benefit to the customer rather than assume a natural interest in what the college is doing.

There is a wide range of promotional channels which can be used in different combinations to achieve optimum cost-effectiveness for different 'products'. The college prospectus, leaflets, advertisements in newspapers and magazines or on the radio, posters, direct mail, personal selling and promotional events can all be effective methods of communicating with potential customers. The unit cost of securing actual enrolments is a crucial indicator of efficiency and it should always be identified as accurately as possible and acted upon.

The maintenance of effective relationships with the media and public is an essential complement to paid-for advertising within the overall promotional strategy. Editorial comment in the media and word of mouth in the local community are potentially the most effective 'advertisements' for the college. If they are unfavourable, they can also jeopardise the results of the rest of the college's publicity programme.

5. Sources of Further Information

Introduction

It is not the intention of this section to provide a comprehensive, let alone exhaustive, set of references on marketing in general or on marketing FHE in particular. Rather, what follows is a select list of sources of further information and addresses which those in FHE, who wish to pursue some of the leads given in the handbook, may find as useful as the authors have found them. A number of texts and reference works are listed, followed by a selection of papers and articles. The section continues with a list of statistical reports produced by the Government and ends with a selection of organisations and their addresses.

Texts and reference works

Kotler, P. **Marketing Management – Analysis, Planning and Control**. Prentice/Hall International Inc. New Jersey. 1980. (Probably the best known and best regarded general marketing text-book).

Kotler, P. **Marketing for Non-Profit Organisations**. Prentice/Hall International Inc. New Jersey. 1982.

Cawthray, B. **Putting it Together: Marketing and Advertising**. Management Learning Productions, Bristol Polytechnic (on behalf of South-West Regional Management Centre). 1982.

Marketing PICKUP. WIGANTECH Publications (on behalf of the Department of Education and Science PICKUP unit), Parsons Walk, Wigan, WN1 1RR. 1985.

The PICKUP Handbook. PICKUP, Department of Education and Science, Room 7/1, Elizabeth House, York Road, London SE1 7PH. 1984.

A Guide to Marketing for Open Tech Projects. Marketing Solutions Ltd. (in association with the Open Tech Unit of the Manpower Services Commission), 70 Salusbury Road, London, NW6 6RJ. 1985.

BRAD (British Rate and Data). Published monthly by McLean-Hunter, 76 Oxford Street, London W1.

The Blue Book of British Broadcasting. Published annually by Tellex Monitors Limited, London WC1X 8RP.

A-Z of Marketing Information Services. Euromonitor Publications Ltd, 87-88 Turnmill Street, London EC1M 5QU.

Marketing Executive Handbook, 11/13 Cricklewood Lane, London, NW2 1ET.

Training Digest. Published monthly by John Chittock, 37 Gower Street, London WC1 6HH.

Key British Enterprises — The top 20,000 British Companies. Dun & Bradstreet, 6-8 Bonhill Street, London EC2 4BU.

Willings Press Guide. Published annually by Thomas Skinner Directories, Windsor Court, East Grinstead House, East Grinstead, W. Sussex RH19 1XE.

Institute of Manpower Studies. **Competence and Competition: Training and Education in the Federal Republic of Germany, the United States and Japan**. National Economic Development Office and the Manpower Services Commission. 1984.

Birch, D. W. & Latcham J. **Managing Open Learning**. Further Education Staff College. 1984.

Government White Paper, **Training for Jobs**. HMSO. 1984.

The Audit Commission Handbook. HMSO. 1983.

<table>
<tr><td>*Papers and articles*</td><td>The Further Education Staff College maintains a large information bank consisting of a number of papers on many aspects of further education. The papers and a select list of them can be obtained from the college's librarian. Some of the papers to which the authors have made reference in the handbook are listed below.</td></tr>
</table>

Cuthbert, R. **The Marketing Function in Education Management**. IBN 1395, FESC, 1979.

Duncan, J. G. **Notes on Marketing Applied to Education**. IBN 1572, FESC, 1980.

Marsh, D. T. **Marketing: A Framework for Action**. IBN 1973, FESC, 1983.

Curtis, J. H. R. **Marketing Further Education: Beginning with a Definition of the Product**. IBN 1939, FESC, 1984.

Foster, J. **Portfolio Analysis in a Polytecnic**. IBN 1974, FESC, 1984.

Cuthbert, R. **Marketing the Department**. IBN 1989, FESC 1984.

Kedney, R. J. **Student Enrolments: Forecasting Trends**. IBN 2037, FESC, 1985.

There are large number of other papers, journals and articles relevant to marketing further education. The authors have found the following useful.

Cassels, J. **Education Training and the Market Place** Unpublished paper, The Association of Colleges for Further and Higher Education, 1984.

Riley, E. 'Marketing Policy and its Cost in a College of Higher Education', **Educational Management and Administration**, Vol. 12, 1984, P217-225.

Brown, J. A. 'The Role of Academic Programs in Institutional Marketing', Marketing Higher Education, **New Directions for Higher Education**, Vol. VI, No. 1, Spring 1978, P1-6.

Mudie, H. C. 'Identifying and Expanding the Desirable Student Pool', Marketing Higher Education, **New Directions for Higher Education**, Vol. VI, No. 1, Spring 1978, P7-22.

Weirick, M. C. 'A Marketing Case History Profile', Marketing Higher Education, **New Directions for Higher Education,** Vol. VI, No. I, Spring 1978 P65-76.

Selby, J. D. 'Marketing Adult Education', **Adult Education,** Vol. 55, No. 3, December 1982 P234-240.

Baldwin, S. 'Publicity and Adult Education', **Adult Education,** Vol. 55, No. 4, March 1983, P364-366.

For those who wish to keep abreast of developments in marketing generally, the following periodicals are recommended:

The Quarterly Review of Marketing. Published by the Institute of Marketing.

CAMPAIGN. Published weekly by Marketing Publications Ltd., 22 Lancaster Gate, London W2 3LY. Available at most newsagents.

Sources of statistical and other detailed information

The following documents, which are published periodically by HMSO, contain much valuable information on educational and employment trends.

Annual Abstract of Statistics

Britain: an Official Handbook

Department of Employment Research

Department of Education and Science Annual Report

✳ **Education Statistics for the UK**

Guide to Official Statistics

United Kingdom National Accounts: the CSO Blue Book

Social Trends

Statistics of education (Volume 3, Further Education).

Organisations supplying useful information

Association of Colleges for Further and Higher Education (ACFHE), Doncaster Metropolitan Institute of Higher Education, High Melton, Doncaster, DN5 7SZ.

Association of Principals of Colleges (APC), Room F108, Garnett College, Downshire House, Roehampton Lane, London SW15 4HR.

British Association of Commercial and Industrial Education (BACIE), 16 Park Crescent. London WIN 4AP.

British Council, 10 Spring Gardens, London, SWIA 2BN.

Central Statistical Office (CSO), Great George Street, London SWI.

Confederation of British Industry (CBI), Centre Point, 103 New Oxford Street, London WCIA IDU.

Communication, Advertising and Marketing Education Foundation (CAM), Ashford House, 15 Wilton Road, London SIV INJ.

College – Employer Links Project (CELP), Elizabeth House, York Road, London SEI 7PH.

Department of Education and Science (DES), Elizabeth House, York Road, London SEI 7PH.

*Further Education Staff College (**FESC**)*, Coombe Lodge, Blagdon, Bristol, BS18 6RG.

*Further Education Unit (**FEU**)*, Elizabeth House, York Road, London, SE1 7PH.

*Institute of Manpower Studies (**IMS**)*, University of Sussex, Mantell Building, Falmer, Brighton, BN1 9RF.

Institute of Marketing, Moor Hall, Cookham, Maidenhead, Berks, SL6 9QH.

*Manpower Services Commission (**MSC**)*, Moorfoot, Sheffield, S1 4PQ. (The Marketing and Information Branch of MSC produces leaflets on Presentations; Handling Objections; Direct Mail; The Telephone; Dealing with the Local Media; Making a Visit).

*National Association of Teachers in Further and Higher Education (**NATFHE**)*, Hamilton House, Mabledon Place, London, WC1H 9BH.

*National Economic Development Office (**NEDO**)*, 21 Millbank, London, SW1.

*Professional, Industrial and Commercial Updating (**PICKUP**)*, Department of Education and Science, Room 7/1, Elizabeth House, York Road, London SE1 7PH.

*Trades Union Congress (**TUC**)*, Congress House, Great Russell Street, London, WC1B 3LS.

Notes

1 *Graham Robinson of Wigan College of Technology is currently undertaking research in this field in relation to PICKUP courses.*

2 *The Action Plan is a scheme which seeks to make FHE in Scotland more flexible and customer orientated. It is based on modularising the provision across all study areas, usually in units of 40 hours, offering wide availability and choice.*

3 *It should be remembered that with most FHE courses, there are the direct customers, or students, and the indirect client-sponsors who may be parents, or employers, or the MSC or some other agency — or several of these at once. Effective marketing strategies have to recognise this and plan accordingly.*

4 *PICKUP (Professional, Industrial and Commercial Up-dating) is the name of the DES initiative designed to follow up its discussion paper* **Continuing Education** *(October 1980) and the response to it.*

5 *Strictly speaking, these are limitations imposed by the design of the* **product** *rather than its delivery system. They have been included in this section, nonetheless, because they all help to restrict the* **availability** *of the products of FHE.*

6 *Although local cable TV networks could well be significant by the end of the 1980s.*